A Gift for

_____

Presented by

_____

YOU KNOW YOU'RE
MIDDLE-AGED
WHEN...

Middle age is when you have stopped growing at both ends and have begun to grow in the middle.

YOU KNOW YOU'RE
MIDDLE-AGED
WHEN...

**Corvettes, Cougars, Chemical Peels,
and Other Ways to Survive Your Midlife Crisis**

ALISON RATTLE AND ALLISON VALE

Reader's
Digest

The Reader's Digest Association, Inc.
Pleasantville, New York/Montreal

To Martyn, Jason, and Anna. All in various stages of the middle ages. Enjoy!
—A.R.

With thanks to Colin, who embraced grumpy middle age long ago.
—A.V.

———∞∞∞———

A READER'S DIGEST BOOK
Copyright © 2010 Michael O'Mara Books Limited
All rights reserved. Unauthorized reproduction, in any manner, is prohibited.
Reader's Digest is a registered trademark of The Reader's Digest Association, Inc.
First published in Great Britain in 2009 by Michael O'Mara Books Limited,
9 Lion Yard, Tremadoc Road, London SW4 7NQ

FOR READER'S DIGEST
U.S. Project Editor: Barbara Booth
Manager, English Book Editorial, Reader's Digest Canada: Pamela Johnson
Project Designer: Elizabeth Tunnicliffe
Senior Art Director: George McKeon
Executive Editor, Trade Publishing: Dolores York
Manufacturing Manager: Elizabeth Dinda
Associate Publisher, Trade Publishing: Rosanne McManus
President and Publisher, Trade Publishing: Harold Clarke

Library of Congress Cataloging-in-Publication Data
Rattle, Alison.
  You know you're middle-aged when-- : cougars, Corvettes, chemical peels,
and other ways to survive your midlife crisis / Alison Rattle and Allison Vale;
illustrations by Louise Morgan.
     p. cm.
  "First published in Great Britain in 2009 by Michael O'Mara Books Limited."
  Includes bibliographical references.
  ISBN 978-1-60652-151-9
  1. Middle age--Humor. 2. Aging--Humor. I. Vale, Allison. II. Title.
  PN6231.M47R38 2009
  818'.602--dc22
                            2009044210

We are committed to both the quality of our products and the service we provide to our
customers. We value your comments, so please feel free to contact us:

The Reader's Digest Association, Inc.
Adult Trade Publishing
Reader's Digest Road
Pleasantville, NY 10570-7000

For more Reader's Digest products and information, visit our website:
www.rd.com (in the United States) • www.readersdigest.ca (in Canada)
Copyright illustrations © Louise Morgan 2009

Printed in the United States of America

1 3 5 7 9 10 8 6 4 2

CONTENTS

INTRODUCTION   6

THE BIG 3-0
Thirty Early Warning Signs   9
of the Onset of "Middle Youth"

YOU KNOW YOU'RE MIDDLE-AGED WHEN...
You're Too Old to Party   15
All You Want Is a Quiet Night at Home   23
You Finally Start Acting Like a Grown-Up   29
It's Time to Dress Your Age   39
You Start Falling Apart   55
The Crisis Finally Strikes   67
You Hit the Big 4-0   75
You Succumb to Midlife Lust   83
Your Eyes Begin to Wander   91
You Feel the Need for Speed   103
You're All a Twitter   111
You Begin Behaving Badly   123
You Say and Do the Dumbest Things   129
It's Time for Something Different   139
Your Sport Turns Extreme   149
You Turn into a Klutz   157
Your Wisdom Saves the Day   165

FOR THE FINAL TIME, FACE IT!
You Know You're Middle-Aged When...   171

Introduction

If you're reading this book, you've most likely noticed an alarming change in your attitude and behavior. Nothing major—no sudden symptoms or wholesale transformations—but simply a creeping suspicion that you're not quite the same person you were, say, five years ago.

Analyzing your recent history, you might even be able to pinpoint the precise moment at which this unnerving condition began to take hold. Perhaps it was when you bought your first home-repair book and stopped driving recklessly. Or that time you lied about being busy in order to stay at home to watch DVDs. How about when that young kid behind the counter called you sir or madam? When you found yourself strangely attracted to a sensible raincoat? Discovered a gray hair? Bought a lovely throw rug? Uttered the ominous words "I can't drink like I used to?"

Okay, breathe. We have good news and bad news for you. The bad news is that you may well be suffering from the early stages of middle age. The good news is that you no longer have to stay out until dawn, dine at McDonald's, look sexy in beachwear, understand the latest Facebook layout, go backpacking, or have the first clue about popular music. You are allowed—expected, no less—to embarrass your children, appreciate the point of opera, wear whatever's comfortable, and complain about "the youth of today." And those are good things, right? Right?

So sit back and make the most of this liberating new phase in life. Embrace your midlife crisis, revel in your right to be stridently opinionated, and take comfort in the knowledge that we may not understand life any better at 40, but we've finally reached the point where we have the guts to admit it.

THE BIG 3-0

Thirty Early Warning Signs of the Onset of "Middle Youth"

1. You leave concerts half an hour before the end to beat the rush.

2. You start buying things like nose-hair clippers, and Tupperware in all shapes and sizes.

3. Instead of throwing out the circular that comes with the Sunday newspaper, you suddenly see both the benefit and the money-saving appeal of the advertised weekly specials.

4. You own a lawn mower. And probably have a winter cover for it, too.

5. You always have enough milk in the fridge and a spare bottle of olive oil in the pantry.

6. When sitting outside a bar, you can't help but admire the establishment's fine hanging baskets.

7. You say things like, "What lovely wallpaper."

8. You own a shed.

9. You spend a whole weekend organizing your shed and then invite your friends over to admire the results.

10. When flicking through the TV channels in search of mindless entertainment, you find yourself unexpectedly drawn to a really interesting documentary about beetles.

11. Before going out anywhere, you check what the parking situation will be.

12. Rather than throwing away old shoes, you keep them in case they come in handy in the yard.

13. You refuse sex with your husband on laundry day, so as not to soil the clean sheets.

14. You stop dreaming of becoming a professional athlete and start dreaming of having a child who might become one instead.

15. You look through the property section before throwing the local newspaper away.

16. You are too exhausted to go out after reading celebrity magazines.

17. You buy your first T-shirt with nothing written on it.

18. You specifically choose restaurants that don't have pictures on the menu.

19. The benefits of a pension scheme suddenly become clear.

20. You are unable to resist the lure of flat-pack self-assembly furniture.

21. You try to be in and out of the restaurants by 11:00 P.M.

22. Pop music suddenly sounds likes a bunch of noise.

23. You no longer get funny looks when you buy a Disney movie or Barbie-themed backpack, because the sales assistant assumes you have children.

24. You find yourself saying, "Whatever happened to…?" and "I remember when we only had three TV channels."

25. You spend whole evenings in hideous themed bars where the music is too loud and the food is too expensive, in the mistaken belief that you haven't turned into your parents.

26. You start to worry about your parents' health.

27. You iron clothes.

28. You complain about "the youth of today."

29. The only person you know who goes to music festivals is your nanny.

30. You come face to face with your own mortality as the indestructibility of your twenties gives way to the realization that if you don't hurry up and settle down soon and have kids, you'll have no one to look after you when you're old and gray and wearing a colostomy bag and you can't go on enjoying yourself like this forever and just think of all the damage you're doing to your body when one quick drink turns into 10 and, wow, did you see you can get 50 percent off a whole set of lifetime-guaranteed cookware when they usually cost at least that much each and they throw in a wok for free and you must remember to plant your bulbs before the ground gets too hard…

> I'm officially middle-aged. I don't need drugs anymore, thank God. I can get the same effect just by standing up real fast.
>
> —*Jonathan Katz*

You're Too Old to Party

Remember when you could party till dawn and still be up for a replay the following night? When hangovers were cured by nothing more than a lazy morning and a sizeable serving of eggs and bacon?

Sure, you can fight your flagging party spirit (armed with coffee and contact lens–friendly eyedrops), but sooner or later we all come to realize that, if we're honest, nothing really beats a night at home watching *Sex and the City* reruns in our pj's. If you recognize yourself in any of these young fogeys, you may just be too old to party.

SLUMBER PARTY

Celebrities have to fight the aging process harder than anyone. When rumors that age was beginning to tame Kate Moss's party spirit, she was prompted to plan a night of debauched revelry. She planned a 34-hour birthday extravaganza for her thirty-fourth birthday, an hour for every year of her life.

Sadly, Kate's best efforts backfired when she collapsed, exhausted, into bed only halfway through the night.

Maybe it's time Kate adopted a bit of midlife wisdom: Try a club soda every other round.

> Middle age is when you still believe you'll feel better in the morning.
>
> —Bob Hope

TOO OLD FOR FOAM?

When journalist Ian Payne of *The Independent* went to Portugal on vacation with his wife, two young children, and friends, the women were wise enough to opt for a relaxing evening on a balmy terrace with a glass or two of chilled wine. The men, however, decided to test out the maxim "You're never too old for a foam party."

"I'd never been to a foam disco before," recalled Ian, "but it seemed like now or never. You know, that feeling of impending midlife crisis when you discover the haircut that makes you look trendy, just as you're getting too old for it." Meanwhile, another foam-induced dilemma for the midlife party animal soon presented itself: Should you wear your glasses or stumble around in the pitch-black and soapy bubbles, partially blind?

But the most alarming discovery that Ian and his companion made during their inaugural—and probably

final—foam-party experience was that the foam fun didn't even start until at least 4:00 A.M. If you're thinking, Good grief, that's long past my bedtime, there's no doubt about it: You're middle-aged.

COMING TO A CLUB NEAR YOU...

Driving along in the car one day, listening to music, Carol, a mother of two, was delighted when one of her favorite tunes came on the radio. Getting into the rhythm and dancing around in her seat to the beat of the music, she turned to her husband and said, "Hey, remember the days when we used to go clubbing? We should do it again sometime."

In the back of the car, the couple's teenage daughter began making retching noises.

"Ugh—you two? Going to a club? You've got to be kidding! You're far too old.... Everyone would just stare at you!"

"Come on," said Carol, "It doesn't have to be a club for teenagers. There must be places for people of our 'slightly more mature years' to go."

"Yeah, there is," said the daughter. "It's called Bingo!"

> **Middle age is having a choice of two temptations and choosing the one that will get you home earlier.**
>
> —*Dan Bennett, comedian*

ARE YOU READY TO ROCK?

At what age should you start thinking about settling for a comfy armchair and a well-selected playlist rather than donning your old Stones T-shirt and throwing a cigarette lighter into your pocket? In other words, how do you know when you're simply too old to rock? Here are a few clues.

→ You check the TV guide before you book your tickets.

→ You don't leave home without your ibuprofen.

➜ You make sure you're well rested before attending the concert.

➜ You no longer balk at bar prices, and you never order the cheapest beer. In fact, as you sip your European pale lager from the bottle, you realize what you really yearn for is a full-bodied Chilean Merlot.

➜ You wonder out loud whether the venue has Wi-Fi.

➜ You snarl because the person in front of you is standing on his seat and you can't see the stage without standing up. And you *really* don't want to have to stand up.

→ You say "I'm pacing myself" and order mineral water between drinks.

→ You have to MapQuest the venue for directions.

→ By 10:30 P.M. you're starting to think it'd be nice if the band wrapped things up and let everyone get home to bed.

→ You don't feel human again until Wednesday.

→ You can't help but worry about health and safety regulations if you see anyone waving a cigarette lighter in time to the music.

→ You're acutely conscious of the singer's grammatical inaccuracies.

→ People stare at you when you dance. And not in a good way.

→ All you can think as your favorite song reaches its climax is, "Why the hell is the floor so sticky?"

> **I hate most of what constitutes rock music, which is basically middle-aged crap.**
>
> *—Sting*

MUDDY MIDDLE AGE

Do you "do" music festivals? Long gone are the days of taking a suspicious three-day leave of absence from school on the pretext of doing volunteer work or suffering from laryngitis, only to return dressed like a hippie and covered in mud. But do you still look forward to dusting off your boots and setting off for one of the summer's biggest festivals?

If the organizer of the world-famous Glastonbury Festival, Michael Eavis, is to be believed, the annual mudfest has very much become the haunt of the "middle youth." Eavis recently bemoaned the aging respectability of his festival-goers and announced that he was looking for ways to entice a younger, hipper audience back to his muddy fields. His fear is that the middle-class thirty- and fortysomethings who increasingly make up the demographic are steadily changing the face of the festival. Forget free-loving hippies: These days, Eavis complained,

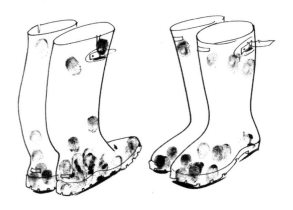

Glastonbury attracts "fantastically well mannered and polite" folk who can easily afford the entrance fee and who generally manage to "grin and bear the mud." Eavis is so convinced the festival needs to tune into a younger vibe that he famously turned down Pink Floyd's David Gilmour on the grounds that he was too old and had little appeal for Eavis's target audience.

The *Daily Mail* was more forthright in its summation of Glastonbury's more, er, mature fans: "The festival has become overrun with middle-aged music lovers who convoy down from the Home Counties in their 4x4s with the desperate hope of clinging on to their youth in a haze of mud and dope smoke."

Eavis says the Internet-only sales drew in the middle class more than the kids, so he plans to hold back about 40 percent of next year's tickets to be sold exclusively through phone sales to give teenagers a chance to buy the tickets via their cell phones. Fans believe this will draw in some of the more "genuine hippies": "You can't expect real hippies to set their alarm for 9:00 A.M. on a Sunday morning and start feverishly hitting refresh on their web browser," said a fan calling himself Fanzine on an Internet chat room discussing the festival.

YOU KNOW YOU'RE MIDDLE-AGED WHEN...

All You Want Is a Quiet Night at Home

Cocooning is the latest marketing buzzword, reflecting a growing trend in twenty-, thirty-, and fortysomethings shunning the bright city lights in favor of curling up at home and having the world come to them. For an increasing number of us, mail-order movie rental + food and drink delivered to the door = a perfect evening.

And it's not just us regular folk who are setting the trend. More and more celebrities will admit to being weary of the big night out. Former Spice Girl Mel B told MTV, "I'm too old for nightclubs....I'm much more into home cooking, dinner parties...that kind of stuff." And *X Factor* judge Cheryl Cole told *OK!* magazine how she detests the fame game so many celebs play at parties: "It's like they're waving across the room, 'Hello, I'm famous, you're famous. I don't really know you but I'm saying hello to you anyway.'" Even "I Kissed a Girl" chart-topper Katy Perry declared that her social life was so quiet it rivaled her grandma's.

HOME CINEMA

The next time you snuggle up for another cozy night in front of your wall-mounted plasma screen, take a moment to consider how your cocoon habit might be affecting your midlife mental health. Try gauging your reaction to some of these unforgettable scenes from Hollywood's finest movies:

When Harry Met Sally
As Meg Ryan fakes her orgasm in a crowded restaurant, is your first thought one of envy and admiration? Are you perhaps intimidated and just a little bit turned on? Or are you utterly distracted by what's in front of her: undoubtedly one of the best-looking sandwiches in cinema history?

The Graduate
As Mrs. Robinson cocks a stockinged leg at gawky college boy Dustin Hoffman and he replies, "Mrs. Robinson, you're trying to seduce me," do you lose yourself in the erotic fantasy, or do you head off to download some Simon & Garfunkel onto your iPod?

Top Gun
As Goose rocks out at the piano to "Great Balls of Fire," are you lost in the beauty of the '80s moment, or are you gripped with nervous tension, yelling, "Get that kid off the piano before he injures himself"?

Saturday Night Fever
Do you wallow in retromania at Travolta's crowd-parting "You Should Be Dancing" moment? Or do you worry about his risk of fungal infection in all that polyester?

Pretty Woman
This is one of those movies that caters to everyone's fantasy, isn't it? For the girls, it's a grown-up Cinderella story with hunky Richard Gere and lashings of old-fashioned seduction. And for the guys it's unlimited wealth and the power to buy yourself a little of what you fancy; in this case, Julia Roberts in a really hot dress. So does *Pretty Woman* float your boat, or does it leave you wincing: Sex on a piano? Ouch! That's gotta hurt!

Titanic
As the unsinkable ship sinks below the icy waves and Leonardo DiCaprio clings manfully to a raft, are you overcome with the tragic unfairness of life, or wondering where on earth Kate Winslet is going to find a decent moisturizer to treat her chapped hands?

Ghostbusters
With New York City saved once again by Dan Aykroyd and Bill Murray, do you breathe a sigh of relief or does all that slimy ectoplasm remind you that you still haven't unblocked the kitchen drain?

WHY LEAVE HOME?

Perhaps one of the most outspoken—if not necessarily the wisest—middle-aged celebrities of modern times is Homer J. Simpson, the antihero of Matt Groening's superb cartoon sitcom *The Simpsons*.

Homer's profound and profane pronouncements about life, love, and beer have worked their way into our daily conversations, but perhaps his most insightful comment is this gem about the futility of leaving the house: "What's the point of going out? We're just going to wind up back here anyway."

> Middle age is when you're sitting at home on a Saturday night and the telephone rings and you hope it isn't for you.
>
> —*Ogden Nash, poet*

> Middle age is having a choice of two
> temptations and choosing the one
> that will get you home earlier.
>
> —*Anonymous*

SIMPLE PLEASURES

Frasier, the NBC sitcom that ran for 11 seasons, was a mine of wisdom and anxiety about the aging process. In "My Coffee with Niles," the episode where Frasier's brother, Niles Crane, reveals the simple pleasures that keep his precarious marriage with the neurotic Maris on track: "Maris and I are old friends. We can spend an entire afternoon together, me at my jigsaw puzzle, she at her autoharp, not a word spoken between us and be perfectly content."

You Finally Start Acting Like a Grown-Up

Take a good look around your home. Are all your houseplants thriving? Do you always have clean underwear? Do you keep a straight face when someone introduces themselves as Dick? Do you choose Fair Trade coffee and organic muesli over Pop-Tarts and chocolate milk? Are you appalled if friends arrive at your door without a bottle of half-decent wine?

Worse still, do you hear yourself churning out the same old lines your parents always did? The ones you swore you'd never use? When you look in the mirror, do you see your mother or father looking back at you?

Can it be happening? Are you finally turning into a grown-up?

FROM SEX AND DRUGS TO SUBURBIA

Growing up happens to us all. Even wild-living rock legends with a penchant for hard drugs and late nights eventually settle down to middle age and the calmness of suburbia.

Bobby Gillespie, front man for the Scottish rock band Primal Scream, is a good example. Known for his hedonistic lifestyle and love affair with drugs—allegedly snorting cocaine while playing table tennis and demanding that his record label open a factory to mass-produce ecstasy—Gillespie hit his forties and moved to the quiet streets of North London with his wife and two young children. Having turned his back on the drugs, he then joined his neighbors in launching a campaign against his local pub's extended music license, complaining that the pub was "playing recorded music at an unacceptable volume past twelve o'clock."

Having once been known to practice the drums by bashing loudly on trash can lids, Gillespie went on to complain that "there was a live percussionist playing along with the records, and the sound was of a very high frequency, which reverberated into my bedroom and my children's bedroom. I found the repetitiveness disturbing, and I was unable to sleep because of it."

Gillespie had his wish granted when the local council ruled that the pub could play loud music late just once a month.

As Jerry M. Wright so wisely pointed out, "The first sign of maturity is the discovery that the volume knob also turns to the left."

TRUE TERROR

Kurt Vonnegut, the acclaimed author of darkly comic sci-fi novels *Cat's Cradle* (1963) and *Slaughterhouse-Five* (1969), knew a thing or two about creating scenes of intense psychological fear. But his own definition of "true terror," he once explained, was to "wake up one morning and discover that your high school class is running the country."

FROM PUNK TO PETUNIAS

Punk rocker Iggy Pop has taken longer than most to reach mellow middle age. Best known for his outrageous onstage antics, which have included flashing his genitals, smearing himself with raw meat and peanut butter, and cutting himself with glass, the Godfather of Punk, it seems, has now turned to gardening and gone all green-fingered.

At London's Chelsea Flower Show in 2007, a garden created by the Children's Society and inspired by Iggy's bestselling *Lust for Life* album, won a silver medal.

"I'm honored," said Iggy, "that the Children's Society's garden is inspired by my music, and I wholeheartedly support the work that they do—they rock."

Rockery and roll!

SIGNS YOU'RE FINALLY GROWING UP

Kitchen

Used to contain   *Now contains*

Case of beer.............................. Bottles of Chardonnay

Hot dogs .... Baby carrots and spinach

Slices of processed cheese.......... Tubs of freshly made
                                          hummus

Cheese-puff snacks .... All-natural multigrain
                                          chips

Half-eaten cans of beans........... Kalamata olives from
                                          the local farmers market

Social Life

Used to go to   *Now go to*

Nightclubs .... Wine bars

Bar .... Dinner with friends

Rock festivals............................ Rock festivals—in a
                                          state-of-the-art
                                          8-passenger SUV

Literature

Used to read	*Now read*
Playboy	Family Handyman
Vogue	Better Homes & Gardens
Harry Potter	Harry Potter—to your children

Shopping

Used to shop at	*Now shop at*
Mini-marts	Local gourmet delis
Ikea	Fashionable department stores
Music store	Hardware store

Furnishings

Used to have	*Now have*
Beanbag chairs	Wraparound couch
A pile of clothes	Walk-in closet with custom shelves
Snack trays	Dining table for six

READING THE SIGNS

Journalist Kerry Williamson, writing in New Zealand's *Dominion Post* in 2009, identified what he saw as the incontrovertible signs of being a grown-up: "I won't get drunk this weekend, I won't perform a naked *haka* on a bar…I won't sleep on someone's couch, I won't enjoy a sneaky cigarette."

Williamson also lamented (or celebrated?) the fact that he was no longer likely to "go dancing and share a cab home with strangers" nor to "wake up on Sunday morning to find a half-eaten pie" next to his bed. Moreover, he concluded that "sleep[ing] until two in the afternoon" and "crank[ing] the stereo to ten" were also things of the past.

It makes youth sound so exhausting, doesn't it?

> **Middle age is the awkward period when Father Time catches up with Mother Nature.**
>
> —*Harold Coffin, humor columnist*

YOU'RE DEFINITELY A GROWN-UP IF...

→ Your houseplants stay alive and you can't smoke any of them.

→ Having sex in a twin bed is out of the question.

→ You find yourself in a garden center and actually recognize the names of some plants.

→ You keep more food than beer in the fridge.

→ Six in the morning is when you get up, not when you go to sleep.

→ You hear your favorite song played in an elevator.

→ You routinely carry an umbrella.

→ You get twitchy if you miss the weather report on TV.

→ Your friends marry and divorce instead of "hook up" and "break up."

→ Jeans and a sweater no longer qualify as "dressed up."

→ You're the one calling the police because those kids next door won't turn down the stereo.

→ Older relatives feel comfortable telling sex jokes around you.

→ You don't know what time the diner closes anymore.

→ Your car insurance goes down and your car payments go up.

→ You feed your dog natural holistic dog food instead of McDonald's leftovers.

→ Sleeping on the couch makes your back hurt.

→ You take naps.

→ A movie and dinner is the whole date instead of the beginning of one.

→ Eating a bucket of KFC at 3:00 A.M. would severely upset, rather than settle, your stomach.

→ You go to the pharmacy for ibuprofen and antacid, not condoms and pregnancy tests.

→ A half-price bottle of French table wine is no longer "pretty good stuff."

➜ You actually eat breakfast food at breakfast time.

➜ "I just can't drink the way I used to" replaces "I'm never drinking again."

➜ Ninety percent of the time you spend in front of a computer is for real work.

➜ You don't save money by drinking at home before going to a bar.

➜ You find out a friend is pregnant and congratulate her rather than holding your hands up in horror and screaming, "Oh, my God, have you told your parents?"

➜ Drinking shots and smoking cigarettes guarantees midnight dry heaves and a sinus attack rather than midnight skinny-dipping and a Big Mac attack.

> **The really frightening thing about middle age is knowing you'll grow out of it.**
>
> —*Doris Day*

YOU KNOW YOU'RE MIDDLE-AGED WHEN...

It's Time to Dress Your Age

Ever cringed at the sight of a middle-aged man parading along the beach in a pair of Speedos? Or winced with embarrassment at the guy in the pub with a beer belly squeezed into a Sex Pistols T-shirt and skin-tight jeans, revealing far more than you thought anatomically possible? Is it possible—*gulp*—that you are one of said specimens?

Guys over 30, listen up: What you could get away with wearing in your late teens and twenties, attire that looked "cool" and "hip" back then, just won't do anymore, especially not when combined with a receding hairline and a few spare pounds around the midriff. It's a hard lesson to learn, but as middle age approaches, the hoodies, scruffy sneakers, and trendy urban gear need to be ditched in favor of a more age-appropriate look and, frankly, a splash of dignity.

MIDDLESCENCE

Writing in the *Daily Telegraph* in 2001, British writer Jeremy Clarkson revealed that he was suffering from "an increasingly common psychological disorder known as 'middlescence,'" which had all the hallmarks of a delayed attack of adolescent behavior.

Clarkson explained that the symptoms of this disorder afflicting middle-aged men included an "uncontrollable urge to dress like a teenager, to party like a teenager and to date women twenty years younger than themselves."

Unfortunately for all you middle-aged men out there, medical science has yet to develop a cure for this alarming condition.

FASHION FAUX-PAS FOR THE
OVER-THIRTIES MAN

1. Tight jeans. In fact, *all* tight pants.

2. High-waisted pants. Yes, you're getting more crotchety, but you're not Simon Cowell.

3. Baseball caps—and it goes without saying that bandanas are definite no-nos. But don't get ahead of yourself and try to graduate to "adult" hats until you've reached your fifties, at which point you can then wear flat caps, Panamas, and fedoras with pride and dignity.

4. Cardigans. These are the sole preserve of the under-twenties, who can wear them with scruffy irony, or the over-sixties, who can legitimately accessorize a beige cardigan with a pipe and slippers.

5. Novelty underwear of any description—particularly thongs or anything involving leopard print.

6. A 20-year-old girl on your arm. Do you want to be a walking cliché?

7. Flip-flops. Unless you live near a beach *and* possess particularly well-groomed feet.

8. Ugg boots. Need we say more?

9. Any T-shirt featuring the bands of your youth.

10. Any T-shirt featuring a current band.

11. Cowboy boots, unless you are Billy Ray Cyrus—and even then ....

12. Denim jackets, unless you are George Michael.

13. Hoodies.

14. Long, thinning hair—especially worn in a ponytail.

15. A deep tan, unless you are Tom Jones or an aspiring lookalike.

16. Brightly colored socks.

17. Skinny-fit T-shirts, cargo pants, pointy shoes, and army surplus–style clothing (unless you are a soldier).

18. Ties that are anything other than tasteful. At your age, you should have acquired a modicum of dignity and should not feel the need to express, via your neckwear, how wild and "wacky" you are.

19. Crocs. What is it with middle-aged men and Crocs? You know, those hideous plastic clogs that come in every color of the rainbow and are strangely reminiscent of the jelly shoes we all had to wear at the beach when we were kids? George W. Bush was photographed wearing them, for goodness' sake! If you absolutely must wear them, only do it in secret. In your shed, perhaps.

20. Speedos, unless you are:
   a) under 30
   b) remarkably toned
   c) a professional swimmer

MIDDLE-AGED MODE

But take heart! There are plenty of new looks you can embrace in your middle years.

→ Tailor-made shirts.

→ Glasses worn halfway down your nose.

→ Cravats or silky scarves, worn in a rakish and eccentric manner.

→ A chef's hat while barbecuing.

→ A good watch.

→ A well-trimmed beard.

→ A confident and slightly aloof facial expression that suggests you are beyond the dictates of fashion.

THE NEED FOR SPEED(O)

A penchant for tight-fitting swimming trunks is a sure sign of the onset of middle age, and yet men who are, shall we say, past the peak of physical fitness continue to wear them. Why? Comedian Tom Papa has the answer.

"I've got a wife and a couple kids," he explains. "I walk to the beach now. I've got diaper bags filled with crap. I'm pulling wagons behind me. No women are looking at me anymore. I figure if I wear the Speedo, they'll be horrified, but at least they'll give me a glance."

Well, so long as there's a logical justification…

> I think men who have a pierced ear are better prepared for marriage. They've experienced pain and bought jewelry.
>
> —Rita Rudner

THE CRISIS WARDROBE

Blogger Piper, writing on the website bestweekever.tv, observes an alarming clothing trend gaining momentum among midlife male A-listers including Tom Cruise, Brad Pitt, and Matthew Fox. Piper writes:

"It's official. The leather biker's jacket is the new symbol of a midlife crisis.... More specifically, the mock-turtleneck-collared, form-fitting Ducati-inspired biker's jacket. More and more male celebrities are sporting this look all over Hollywood. The aerodynamic collar and sharp darted shoulders are designed to give the impression that these aging celebs can rock climb, drag race or leap from explosions at a moment's notice—'cause their lives are just that crazy."

THE EVOLUTION OF FASHION

The BBC's version of the hilariously candid sitcom *Men Behaving Badly* followed the lives and loves of two thirtysomethings, Gary and Tony, who shared a flat in London.

In one episode Gary laments his inevitable decline from youth to dull middle age: "I was a schoolboy, then I was an office junior, then I became a new office manager, then I joined the Floppy Knitwear scene."

MUTTON DRESSED AS LAMB

There comes a moment in every woman's life when she realizes she's well and truly arrived at middle age, and it's not always the appearance of that first gray hair or the creeping crow's feet that forces the truth upon her, either. It can hit a woman unexpectedly—when out bra shopping, for example, when the sales assistant tactlessly steers her away from the sexy, lacy numbers toward the firm-control all-in-one foundation garments: the "I am never going to have sex again" genre of lingerie.

But don't ditch your entire wardrobe and replace it with beige slacks and elasticized waists *just yet*. You have a few decades of stylish middle age to enjoy first.

> **Looking 50 is great—if you're 60.**
>
> —*Joan Rivers*

FASHION FAUX-PAS FOR THE
OVER-THIRTIES WOMAN

1. Tight pants that give you an overspill are a definite no-no. Especially anything that's tight around the crotch.

2. Velour sweatsuits.

3. Ugg boots.

4. Velour sweatsuits worn with Ugg boots.

5. Neon or highly patterned leggings.

6. Frayed denim miniskirts that barely skim your behind.

7. Thigh-high vinyl boots à la Julia Roberts in *Pretty Woman*. Trust us, you will look like a fisherman.

8. Cropped tops that show off your stomach. Even if you do have a six-pack.

9. Leopard print. In fact, anything animal-inspired.

10. Culottes. Although, admittedly, no one of any age can get away with these.

11. Ditto underwear that is so big or so small that it pokes out from the top of your pants.

12. Anything with any see-through element whatsoever, including, but not limited to, fishnet stockings.

13. T-shirts featuring cartoon characters beloved by 10-year-old girls (Barbie, Hello Kitty… the list is endless).

14. Unnaturally long nails, unless you're trying to lure Hansel and Gretel into a gingerbread house.

15. Ill-fitting shoes, especially if they are very high, very pointy, and redolent of an exotic dancer.

16. A belly-button piercing.

17. Hot pants. Kylie Monogue can get away with it, but we suspect she may be immortal.

18. Orange-tinted foundation. Leave that to eighteen-year-olds who don't know any better.

19. Ditto spiderlike mascara and enthusiastically applied eyeshadow.

20. Blouses buttoned up to the neck, worn with a lovely brooch. You're middle-aged, not past it.

IT'S ALL ABOUT INK

Nowadays it seems no midlife crisis is complete unless it is commemorated in ink.

British *Big Brother* presenter Davina McCall revealed in an interview with the *Daily Telegraph* that she planned to mark her fortieth birthday with another tattoo.

"I'm going to get my fifth tattoo with a fifty-eight-year-old friend who's never had one. I want to get something sci-fi or Gothic, but I'm very open to new ideas. I've always been a real sci-fi geek, and I've already got an alien on my bottom. But there is one tattoo I want to get covered first; it's a chili, but whenever I show it to anyone, they think it's a carrot, so it has got to go."

> I wear glasses so I can look for
> things I keep losing.
> —*Bill Cosby*

FOREVER ON MY ARM

The first throes of passion will all too often drive us to declare our love in indelible ink, carved onto chest, arm, or butt. Actor Johnny Depp was moved to do just that after meeting and falling in love with Winona Ryder on the set of *Edward Scissorhands.* As testament to their enduring love, Depp had the words WINONA FOREVER tattooed on his arm. Three years later, the relationship over, Depp had the tattooist knock up a quick rewrite. The tattoo now reads WINO FOREVER.

Perhaps Depp should have heeded the advice of comedienne Carol Leifer, who once recommended that "if you plan on having your lover's name tattooed on your arm, always leave room before it for a possible 'I Hate' down the road."

NAMES IN STRANGE PLACES

America's best-known forensic pathologist is Michael
Baden, former chief medical officer of New York and a
familiar face on HBO's *Autopsy*. In his career as a coroner,
he has performed thousands of autopsies. Former *Late
Night* TV host Conan O'Brien once asked him what
had been the strangest tattoo he'd ever seen on a corpse.
Baden replied that the tattoo in question appeared on a
man's butt.

Asked what it read, he replied, "Your name."

"Conan?"

"No. 'Your name.'"

It transpired that this particular guy had spent a lot
of his time hanging out in bars and winning free drinks
off strangers by betting them he had their name ("your
name") tattooed on his backside.

The only thing you have to focus on
in your twenties is not getting a bad tattoo.
You don't want to be forty going,
"No dude, it was different back then.
Everyone loved SpongeBob—everyone."

—*Tom Papa*

THE WRITING ON THE WALL

It's not often that you hear of a divorce being the subject of a new tattoo. But when rap artist Eminem filed for divorce from his first wife, Kim Mathers, in 2000, she accepted that her marriage was over. When your husband gets himself a new tattoo saying KIM—ROT IN PIECES, it really is time to move on.

> Women, don't get a tattoo. That butterfly looks great on your breast when you're twenty or thirty, but when you get to seventy, it stretches into a condor.
>
> —*Billy Elmer*

IN THE NAME OF LOVE

To celebrate 15 glorious years of blissful marriage to his wife, Lisa, Welshman Alan Jenkins decided to get a commemorative tattoo. He spent over 20 agonizing hours in a tattoo parlor having the tribute to his wife created. The design also included portraits of their daughters and cost Alan nearly $1,650.

Unfortunately for Alan, no sooner had the ink dried than his wife admitted she had been having an affair and was leaving him to shack up with her 25-year-old fitness trainer.

Looking on the bright side, Alan said of his wife, "She may have left me, but she'll be with me forever, thanks to the tattoo. And I've still got room on my chest if I get hooked up again."

TO B OR NOT TO B

A woman, frustrated with her love life because her husband is obsessed with Brigitte Bardot and ignores her completely, tried to win back his attentions by going to a tattooist to have the letters BB tattooed on her breasts. The tattooist warned her that age and gravity would have an unfortunate effect on this look later in life and suggested she have the letters tattooed on her bottom instead. She agreed and allowed him to ink a B on each buttock. When her husband came home from work that night, she turned around, lifted up her dress, and bent over to show him the artwork.

"What do you think?" she asked.

"Huh?" he replied. "Who the hell is Bob?"

You Start Falling Apart

It's no secret that more middle-aged women than ever are turning to cosmetic surgery in a bid to hold back the years. Botox at breakfast, liposuction at lunchtime, and dermabrasion for dinner have become the norm. Even someone as enviably young-looking as Gwyneth Paltrow is allegedly smearing snake venom on her blemish-free complexion to ward off the first signs of wrinkles.

Men, on the other hand, have always been only too happy to slide comfortably into middle age, occasionally swapping their wife and children for an electric guitar and a ponytail when they hit the big 4-0.

Until now, that is. Plastic surgeons are reporting a huge rise in business as a new phenomenon known as the "menopaunch" has middle-aged men by the thousands lining up in the surgeon's waiting room to have the fat sucked from their bulging waistlines and man boobs, as well as their sagging jowls lifted, eye bags removed, and receding hairlines un-receded.

COMING UNDONE

Writing in *The Independent* in 2008, journalist Toby Young recalled the first time he realized he was past his prime.

"One of my shoelaces had come undone," he explained, "and I was about to bend down to tie it up when I thought, Hang on. If I wait until the other one comes undone, I'll only have to bend over once to tie up both laces."

Does this sound embarrassingly familiar? As Young concluded, "Once you begin strategizing to reduce the number of times you'll have to bend down, your salad days are over."

HAIRS AND GRACES

Writer Stephen J. Lyons says about his new obsession with rogue hairs: "Eyebrows that I once never gave a second thought to have turned against me. If I am lax with the razor for even a day, a rapid-response rebel hair will break off from the more conservative eyebrow community and strike out north on its own."

So is this what the middle years are all about, then? Plucking, tweezing, shaving, jogging, and squeezing into lycra at the gym? Fighting every gray hair and new wrinkle with an array of ever more bizarre lotions and potions that promise eternal youth? Or should we just give up on it all and fall apart?

It's a dilemma understood all too well by comedy writer J. R. Havlan, who laments, "I don't even have hair anymore—I have hairs. Do you understand the difference? When you have hair, you can style it. When you have hairs, you can count them."

> **To get back my youth I would do anything
> in the world, except take exercise,
> get up early, or be respectable.**
>
> —*Oscar Wilde*, The Picture of Dorian Gray

BALD BUT BRAINY

Little Jack was in a thoughtful mood as he ate his breakfast one morning.

"Mom," he said, "why has dad only got a few hairs on his head?"

"Hmmmm..." said his mother, trying to think fast. "Well, it's because he's so very clever."

"Oh," said Jack, "so why do you have so much hair, then?"

FACE-OFF

The list of middle-aged signs of decay is seemingly endless, spanning everything from gray hair to the need for reading glasses, and from a bad back to crow's feet (or laughter lines, as we prefer to call them).

Mil Millington, author of the novel *Things My Girlfriend and I Have Argued About*, has another entry to add to the list: "At forty-two," he says, "your skin begins to hint that an over-vigorous wash could easily result in your face falling off into the sink."

Now there's something we hadn't thought to panic about just yet....

YOUTH IS WASTED ON THE YOUNG

"How did it happen?" the doctor asked the middle-aged farmhand as he set the man's broken leg.

"Well, doc, twenty-five years ago..."

"Never mind the past. Tell me how you broke your leg this morning."

"Like I was saying, twenty-five years ago I had my first day of work on the farm. That night, right after I'd gone to bed, the farmer's beautiful daughter came into my room and asked me if there was anything I wanted. I said, 'No thanks, everything is fine.' 'Are you sure?' she asked; 'I'm sure,' I said. 'Isn't there anything I can do for you?' she persisted; 'I reckon not,' I replied."

"Excuse me," said the doctor, "but what does this story have to do with your leg?"

"Well, this morning," the farmhand explained, "when it finally dawned on me what she meant, I fell off the roof."

> Youth is a wonderful thing. What a crime to waste it on children.
>
> —George Bernard Shaw

KNOCKING OFF THE YEARS

Susan got knocked over by a car on her thirty-fifth birthday. She was rushed to a hospital and, while on the operating table, had a near-death experience: God appeared before her.

She asked him, "Well, is this it for me, then?"

God replied, "Oh, no. You easily have another thirty or forty years to live."

After recovering from her injuries, Susan decided to stay on at the hospital and have a few cosmetic procedures: a breast augmentation, liposuction, collagen injections, and a facelift. If she was going to live for another 30 or 40 years, she figured she may as well make the most of it.

A couple of weeks later, she left the hospital feeling— and looking—like a 20-year-old again. As she walked out the doors, she was knocked over and killed by a speeding ambulance.

Arriving in front of God, she shouted angrily, "Hey! I thought you said I had another thirty or forty years?"

"Good grief!" God replied. "I'm so sorry, Susan, but I didn't recognize you!"

BYPASSING MIDDLE AGE

A woman walked up to a little old man rocking in a chair on his porch. "I couldn't help noticing how happy you look," she said. "What's your secret for a long, happy life?"

"I smoke three packs of cigarettes a day," he said. "I also drink a case of whisky a week, eat fatty foods, and never exercise."

"That's amazing!" exclaimed the woman. "How old are you?"

"Twenty-six."

LOSING PERSPECTIVE

As most of us have by now convinced ourselves, age is just a number. Instead of obsessing over hitting 40, we should keep things in perspective and look for the silver lining.

But every silver lining hides a cloud, as comedian Tracy Smith so eloquently illustrates: "Twenty-two-year-old boy sees me naked, he'll go, 'Well, that's what an older woman looks like, I guess.' Twenty-two-year-old girl sees me naked, she'll go, 'I better start taking care of myself. Never too early to moisturize.'"

FACE FACTS

Other celebrities are less squeamish at the thought of facial enhancement. Opera singer Lesley Garrett once admitted to having botox but preempted criticism by pointing out that "everyone in the world has botox. My cat has botox."

Meanwhile, *X Factor* and *American Idol* judge Simon Cowell is less apologetic about the increasingly popular procedure. "To me," he said, "botox is no more unusual than toothpaste."

FACE-LIFT FUROR

A woman in her forties went to a plastic surgeon for a face-lift. The surgeon told her about a new procedure called the Knob, where a small knob is placed on the back of a woman's head and, when turned, tightens up her skin to produce the effect of a brand-new face-lift. Of course, the woman handed over her cash and demanded to have the Knob installed at once.

Over the course of the years, the woman tightened the knob and the effects were fantastic: She remained young-looking and vibrant. But after 15 years, she returned to the surgeon with two problems.

"All of these years, everything has been working just fine. I've had to turn the knob many times, but I've always been very happy with the results. But now I've developed two annoying problems. First, I have these terrible bags under my eyes, and the knob just won't get rid of them."

The doctor looked at her closely and said, "Those aren't bags, those are your breasts."

The woman sighed and said, "Well, I guess there's no point in asking about the goatee...."

> Hair is the first thing. And teeth the second. A man's got those two things, he's got it all.
>
> —James Brown

GUESS MY AGE

A middle-aged woman decided to treat herself to a face-lift for her birthday. She forked over thousands but loved the results. A while later she's on her way home from work when she stops to buy a newspaper. After paying, she says to the assistant, "I hope you don't mind my asking, but how old do you think I am?"

"About thirty," comes the reply.

"Actually, I'm forty-eight," says the woman delightedly, and saunters out of the shop.

Feeling a little hungry, the woman goes into a fast-food restaurant. She asks the girl behind the counter, "So, how old do you think I am?"

"I'd say around twenty-eight," says the girl.

"Wrong!" says the woman. "I'm exactly forty-eight, would you believe!"

She skips away, feeling really good about herself.

Next, the woman goes into a pharmacy to buy some perfume and again feels the urge to ask the sales assistant the same question.

"I would guess you were around thirty," says the assistant.

"Well, I'm actually forty-eight!" the woman replies proudly. "But thank you so much."

She floats out of the shop and heads to the bus stop. There's an old man waiting there, and the woman can't resist asking her question one more time.

"Well," says the old man, "I'm eighty now, and my eyesight's not what it used to be, but in my younger days I knew of a foolproof way to tell a lady's age. You might think it's a bit strange, but I'll have to put my hand up under your bra. I'll be able to tell exactly how old you are then."

The woman thinks for a moment. Looking around, she realizes the street is empty and decides to give the old man a chance to guess her age. He puts both his hands under her shirt and then inside her bra, caressing her breasts and looking thoughtful.

After a while the woman says, "Okay, Okay, that's enough now. So come on, how old am I?"

The old man removes his hands from her breasts and says, "Madam, you are exactly forty-eight years old."

The woman is amazed. "But how could you possibly know that just from feeling my breasts?" she asks.

The old man replies, "I can't. I was in line behind you at the fast-food joint."

CRACKING UP

Lynne Truss, best-selling author of *Eats, Shoots and Leaves*, has made an alarming connection between spotting the first signs of physical decay and generally becoming a middle-aged grump. In 2005's *Talk to the Hand*, Truss pinpoints the moment at which a person begins the descent into grouchiness.

"Check out your...elbow skin," she writes. "If it just sits there in a puckered fashion, a bit rough and belligerent, then you can probably also name about twenty things, right now, off the top of your head, that drive you nuts."

> I guess I don't mind so much being old, as I mind being fat and old.
>
> —*Peter Gabriel*

YOU KNOW YOU'RE MIDDLE-AGED WHEN...
The Crisis Finally Strikes

For a while you can tell yourself that you are at ease with who you are and that aging holds no fears. But sooner or later, there will come a time when you wake up in the small hours in a cold sweat, sick with the realization that the best days of your youth are pretty much played out. You start wondering whether now's the time to take that year out to travel the world, or to renew your lapsed gym membership, or to make a move on the office hottie, or toy with a nipple piercing or a back wax....

This is the classic onset of the midlife crisis, an unsettling phenomenon that you denounce as a comic cliché until you have one of your own. Once you detect the early signs of your own MLC, brace yourself; things will get a whole lot worse before they get better. As someone rather morbidly once said, the worst thing about a midlife crisis is the knowledge that you are only halfway through all the shit that life's going to throw at you.

YOU'RE ON THE VERGE
OF A MIDLIFE CRISIS WHEN...

→ You kiss your wife and she yawns.

→ Your six-pack turns to a one-pack.

→ At weddings, when everyone gets up to dance, you are asked to watch the table.

→ You appreciate that quality is more important than quantity.

→ You have to nap for 30 minutes after running half a mile and doing 10 sit-ups.

→ Watching TV until midnight constitutes "letting your hair down."

→ You start making that special old-man groaning noise when getting up from a chair.

→ You realize that caution is the only thing you care to exercise.

→ You realize you're already halfway through your working life.

→ You buy your first pair of sensible slippers.

➔ You realize that you're still only halfway through your working life.

➔ Someone recommends their cosmetologist/plastic surgeon/anti-wrinkle cream to you.

➔ You make an appointment with a cosmetologist/ plastic surgeon, just in case the anti-wrinkle cream doesn't work.

➔ Your parents give up asking you when you're going to make something of yourself and begin nagging your children instead.

➔ Your boss is younger than you.

➔ Your doctor is younger than you.

➔ You have no idea who half the people in gossip magazines are, let alone why millions of people would pay good money to read about them.

➔ You refer to twentysomethings as "young people."

➔ Most of the people in your wedding album have divorced.

> My mother used to say, "The older you get, the better you get. Unless you're a banana."
>
> —*Betty White*, The Golden Girls

WHAT MIDLIFE CRISIS?

In 2002 activist and U2 star Bono caused a stir among music-industry pundits and gossip columnists alike when the lyrics of his new track "New York" indicated that he might be undergoing a midlife crisis. The song included the lines, *I'm staying on to figure out my midlife crisis. I hit an iceberg in my life, but you know I'm still afloat.* Was this really a frank and open admission of a man in trouble? Bono was dismissive, telling *Q* magazine, "Everyone who knows me knows that I had a midlife crisis when I was about twenty-seven."

THE COST OF A MIDLIFE CRISIS

For all you men out there in your thirties and forties, here's some sobering information that may just stop you from rushing headlong into your midlife crisis. Have you ever thought what it costs to recapture your youth? What it costs to deny the onset of middle age? Well, according to a recent survey, men between the ages of 30 and 49 spend, on average, nearly $40 billion every year in an effort to hold back the signs of aging. Here's what they spend it on:

Dream-chasing vacations	$18 billion
Cool gadgets	$4 billion
Beauty products	$3.8 billion
Trendy clothes	$3.7 billion
Keeping fit	$3.5 billion
Cars/motorcycles	$2.4 billion
Going to trendy bars with younger people	$1.7 billion
Keeping up with contemporary music	$1.4 billion
Viagra, etc.	$713 million
Cosmetic treatments	$489 million

TOTAL   **approximately $39 billion**

If you're still desperate to cling to the vestiges of your youth, you'd better make sure that your wallet is fat.

MLC ON THE BIG SCREEN

Loads of movies have been produced about men and women searching for happiness in a life that they suddenly realize has become a continuous climb on the down escalator. Plots that feature characters reexamining their lives and wondering where they would be "if they had just taken that other road" are not new but, if done properly, are always a box-office draw, possibly because so many 30-and-overs can relate.

Here are just a few of the winners:

Wild Hogs (2007) A hilarious comedy about a group of middle-aged friends who decide to take a break from their stressful jobs and routine family responsibilities to don their motorcycle helmets and find freedom on the open road.

City Slickers (1991) A sentimental but amusing comedy filled with one-liners starring Billy Crystal, who plays an urban radio station sales executive in the throes of a midlife crisis. For his birthday he, along with two friends, decides to participate in a two-week cattle drive from New Mexico to Colorado. While there, the three city slickers are challenged by humorous mishaps and begin to resolve their midlife dilemmas.

American Beauty (1999) A drama about forty-two-year-old Lester Burnham, who is falling deeper and deeper into a depression trying to deal with his super-arrogant bitch-on-wheels wife and his rebellious, self-absorbed daughter. One day he meets one of his daughter's friends and becomes so infatuated with her that he quits his high-paying job to work in a fast-food restaurant so he can get to know her better and relive his youth.

Middle Age Crazy (1980) When Bobby Lee, played by Bruce Dern, realizes that his fortieth birthday is just around the corner, he begins to see that his life is not what he had envisioned: His wife has lost some of her appeal, and his friends and family are treating him like he's over the hill. After his father dies, he loses it and hooks up with a Dallas Cowboy Cheerleader, trading in his business suit for cowboy boots.

> **Only the lottery or premature death can save me now.**
>
> —*Dorothy*, Men Behaving Badly

YOU KNOW YOU'RE MIDDLE-AGED WHEN...

You Hit the Big 4-0

Does life seem to have become just a little bit bleaker since you turned 40? Or perhaps you're still in your thirties and break into involuntary muscle spasms whenever anyone mentions the big 4-0? If so, it may offer you a little comfort to know that you are not alone. Studies have revealed that, across 72 countries worldwide, we all dread turning 40.

It seems that, regardless of culture, we experience a universal low in our sense of well-being after the event; effectively it is now that we linger temporarily at the bottom of a sort of U-bend of happiness.

AGING GRATEFULLY

While many women dread the day they wake up to find themselves looking "the wrong side of 30," crime writer Agatha Christie, creator of the popular fictional detectives Miss Marple and Hercule Poirot, found a novel way around the problem of aging.

At age 40, and following a failed first marriage to unfaithful aviator Archie Christie, Agatha married Max Mallowan, an archaeologist.

"An archaeologist is the best husband any woman can have," she once declared, explaining, "the older she gets, the more interested he is in her."

STUFF THAT HAPPENS WHEN A GUY TURNS 40

→ Nothing makes him quake with terror more than a dance floor.

→ He starts drinking his veggies and builds a gym in the garage.

→ He talks back to every referee, political commentator, and quiz contestant on TV. And he's always right.

→ His colleagues think it's okay to make Viagra jokes.

→ He secretly worries his colleagues might have a point about the Viagra.

→ He quietly sneers at every young person he sees wearing a hoodie but crosses the road anyway, just in case.

→ He starts to learn the electric guitar...

→ ...and takes up Tae Kwon Do. At least until it starts to hurt.

→ He gets irate whenever anyone talks about "emotional closure."

→ He wants to punch everyone who orders lunch with the phrase, "Can I get..."

YOU ARE NOT ALONE

If the thought of turning 40 has you quaking in your ill-advised Ugg boots, take heart from the fact that millions of others have gone through the same trauma before you. That said, people approach the ominous date in very different ways.

While Jennifer Aniston told *People* magazine that she was "very excited" to be over the follies of youth—"what I wish I'd known when I was thirty!"—Daniel Craig, Mr. 007, admitted that "turning forty meant less to [him] than [he] thought it would." However, his lack of enthusiasm might have had something to do with the fact that he woke up with a hangover on his birthday: "It wasn't a pretty sight."

Some people use their newfound age to take stock of the harsh realities of life—Jeremy Clarkson wrote in the *Daily Telegraph* that he was horrified to find himself "forty, unbelievably ugly, a colossal bore, and as money-oriented as a salesman in a cell phone shop"—while others

take a more philosophical approach to things. British comedian and political activist Mark Steel, writing in *The Independent,* pointed out that things become even more finite the older we get.

"If you average one foreign holiday a year you've probably got about thirty-five left," he explained. "Even bananas—at, say, two a week, you're down to roughly your last 3,600, so a disappointing banana now carries a poignancy that didn't apply at nineteen."

GETTING ON

When Harry Met Sally, the 1989 movie written by Nora Ephron and directed by Rob Reiner, is the story of a meant-to-be couple as they develop from stubborn studenthood into mellow middle age. The film is packed full of hilarious quips about getting older, but this is our favorite exchange.

Sally: I drove him away. AND I'm gonna be forty.
Harry: When?
Sally: Someday.
Harry: In eight years.
Sally: But it's there. It's just sitting there, like some big dead end. And it's not the same for men. Charlie Chaplin had kids when he was seventy-three.
Harry: Yeah, but he was too old to pick them up.

ROLLING BACK THE YEARS

A man asked his wife, "What would you most like for your fortieth birthday?"

She said, "It's totally impossible, but I'd love to be ten again."

On the morning of her birthday, the husband got her up bright and early and whisked her off to a theme park. He put her on every single ride in the park, from the Death Slide to the Screaming Loop, via the Wall of Fear.

Four hours later, her head reeling and her stomach churning, the wife was bundled back into the car and taken, blindfolded, to a special restaurant: McDonald's. Here, the husband sat her down and brought her a Double Big Mac with extra fries and a chocolate shake.

They then went to the movie, where the wife was treated to popcorn, lemonade, and more candy than she had ever seen in her life.

At last the wife staggered home with her husband and collapsed into bed, utterly exhausted by her day. Her husband leaned over and asked, "Well, dear, what was it like being ten again?"

There was a silence; then one eye opened and she groaned, "Actually, darling, I meant dress size ten."

A SOBERING THOUGHT

Did you ever notice that the roman numerals for 40 are XL?

BIRTHDAY TRUTHS

For his wife's fortieth birthday party, Carl ordered a cake with this inscription: "You are not getting older. You are just getting better."

When the baker asked how he wanted it arranged, Carl told him, "Just put 'You are not getting older' at the top, and 'You are just getting better' at the bottom."

It wasn't until the cake was wheeled out in front of hundreds of friends and relatives that Carl noticed the inscription: "You are not getting older at the top. You are just getting better at the bottom."

> I'm not forty, I'm eighteen with twenty-two years' experience.
>
> —*Anonymous*

You Succumb
to Midlife Lust

If you think your libido takes a nosedive sometime after your thirtieth birthday and it's only the twentysomethings with their perfectly toned flesh who are getting all the raunchy action, think again. Contrary to popular belief, sex in the "middle ages" is alive, kicking, and as spicy and as passionate as ever. Hooray for being over 30!

Surveys from all over the world show time and time again that sex in your forties is the best ever; women in their forties in particular want to have sex much more often than their younger counterparts.

As comedian Jimmy Carr so shrewdly confirms, "Women reach their sexual peak after thirty-five years. Men reach theirs after about four minutes."

THANKS, BUT NO THANKS

Dashing movie star Tony Curtis once volunteered to participate in a "Win Tony Curtis for a Weekend" contest.

"They gave me away as a prize," he recalled. "The woman who won was disappointed. She'd hoped for second prize: a new stove."

THERAPEUTIC GARDENING

A gardener from Preston, Maine, struck upon a novel way of boosting his business when he offered to work in the nude. His phone didn't stop ringing, with bored middle-aged housewives clamoring to book him for his trimming skills. Thirty-three-year-old Phil charged extra for

stripping—a service that proved to be a huge moneymaker for his fledgling business.

"They invite friends round for a bit of a laugh, and there is a lot of peeping through the curtains. I do not mind stripping off at all. You feel nice and free without the restriction of clothes, but you do have to watch out for some of the prickly bits. We use a lot of power tools, too, so I am always aware of the dangers."

DAILY BREAD

Two middle-aged men, Paul and John, are chatting on a park bench when Paul cautiously asks John about his sex life. John answers proudly that he has an excellent sex life and is still very active. Embarrassed, Paul confesses that his sexual appetite seems to be waning somewhat and asks John if he has any secrets for staying sexually vital.

"Well," answered John, "I eat rye bread every day. That's my secret. If you just eat rye bread, your sex life will improve dramatically."

Paul decides to follow this advice and finds a nearby bakery. He tells the baker that he wants every loaf of rye bread that they have in stock.

The baker asks him, "Do you want whole loaves or do you want us to slice them?"

Paul looks puzzled and asks the baker, "What is the difference?"

"When it's sliced," says the baker, "it gets hard faster."

Paul is astounded. "How come everyone knew about this but me?"

> You can't go on and on for hours—at least not without putting your back out.
>
> —*Geoffrey Wansall, author*

DON'T THROW IN THE TOWEL

A middle-aged man marries a younger woman but discovers that no matter what he does in bed, she won't have an orgasm. He takes the problem to his doctor, who tells him that fantasy may be the answer. So the man hires a young, toned male escort and has him stand naked and gently fanning a giant palm leaf over the couple while they make love. Still his wife doesn't orgasm.

The man returns to the doctor, who now suggests he reverse the scene: The escort should have sex with the wife while the husband fans the palm leaf.

The man duly returns home to try out the doctor's suggestion. Sure enough, his wife is soon overcome by throes of noisy passion. Tapping the escort on the shoulder, the husband cries in triumph, "See, *that's* how you fan a damn leaf!"

> Middle age is when a guy keeps turning off lights for economical rather than romantic reasons.
>
> —*Lillian Gordy Carter*

WHEN IT ALL GOES HORRIBLY WRONG

A middle-aged truck driver was fortunate enough to marry a gorgeous woman half his age. On their honeymoon, he soon discovered, to his great embarrassment, that he could not last long enough to satisfy his young bride in bed. Although his wife was tender and reassuring, such was the truck driver's humiliation that he was determined to visit a doctor on his return from their honeymoon.

"Doctor," he pleaded, "I have a young and very sexy wife, but I can't hold back long enough to satisfy her when we make love. Is there anything I can do?"

The doctor nodded in a knowing way, patted him on the back, and said, "The next time you plan to have intercourse with your wife, try a bit of self-stimulation first. I can guarantee that you'll last longer and will be able to satisfy her completely."

The truck driver agreed to give it a go. Later that day, his wife called him at work to say that she was feeling frisky and would be tearing his clothes off the moment he walked through the door.

The time had come for him to take the doctor's advice. But where should he do the deed? At his office? In a public toilet? What if someone walked in on him? He got into his truck to begin the journey home. Then the idea came to him: He would find a quiet spot on the road, pull over, climb underneath the truck, pretend to be inspecting the exhaust, and then follow the doctor's advice there.

A short while later he was lying under his truck with his eyes tightly closed, visualizing his gorgeous young wife, when he felt someone tugging on his pant leg. Reluctant to ruin the fantasy he was enjoying, he kept his eyes shut and asked, "Yes, what do you want?"

"Sir, I'm a police officer. Can you tell me what you're doing, please?"

"Yes, officer," the man replied confidently. "I'm just inspecting my truck's exhaust."

"Well, I suggest you check the brakes while you're at it. Your truck rolled down the hill a few minutes ago."

A BIT OF SPICE IN THE KITCHEN

Celebrity chef Jamie Oliver knows the importance of keeping a marriage alive. He routinely does the cooking at home and decided to spice things up a little one Valentine's Day. He prepared a beautiful roast for his wife, the lovely Jools, and served dinner butt naked.

Unfortunately, the self-styled Naked Chef learned the importance of dressing for dinner the hard way when he burned his own "meat and two veg" on the oven door.

"It really ruined my evening," Oliver remembered later, "… and my night."

> One of the best parts of growing older?
> You can flirt all you like since you've
> become harmless.
>
> —*Liz Smith*

STAMP COLLECTING

A middle-aged man and woman meet, fall in love, and decide to get married. On their wedding night, as they settle into the bridal suite at their hotel, the bride says to her new groom, "Please promise to be gentle; I'm still a virgin."

The startled groom says, "How can that be? You've been married three times before."

The bride responds, "Well, you see, it was this way: My first husband was a psychiatrist, and all he ever wanted to do was talk about it. My second husband was a gynecologist, and all he ever wanted to do was look at it. And my third husband was a stamp collector, and all he ever wanted to do was...God, I miss him!"

A MANLY CUP OF TEA

Many male actors reach a certain age and feel an urge to prove they still have what it takes to turn heads. A wheat-grass diet and an intense workout program later, they're suddenly ready to play the mature romantic lead, savoring those lingering close-ups in steamy bedroom scenes. Bare-all photo shoots are another favorite.

But when *X-Files* actor David Duchovny agreed to pose naked for a magazine, it seems he had a last-minute change of heart, grabbing the nearest object at hand, a coffee mug, to cover his manhood.

His wife, Téa Leoni, was not amused, telling David that he was "an idiot." More important, as David later revealed, "she vowed never to drink out of that mug again!"

> A man's only as old as the woman he feels.
>
> —*Groucho Marx*

WOMANLY WILES

In her first bloom of midlife, Barbra Streisand was known to dabble in foreign affairs. Her unconventional approach to international diplomacy didn't go unnoticed. Former secretary of state Henry Kissinger once remarked, "She has outdone me....Could I have greeted [Serbian dictator] Slobodan Milosevic by saying, 'Hello, Gorgeous?' Could I have flicked my perfectly manicured fingers at his temples and said, 'In my country, powerful men seldom have such thick hair?' I think not."

YOU KNOW YOU'RE MIDDLE-AGED WHEN...
Your Eyes Begin to Wander

It's a common enough situation: You have the perfect partner, the perfect home, a great job, and a couple of beautiful kids. Then one day—usually sometime between your thirtieth and fortieth birthdays—you wake up and suddenly the job's boring, the kids are growing up, you've had it with DIY weekends, and your partner is looking decidedly frayed around the edges. To top it off, your hair is thinning, your waist is expanding, and you've started wearing pajamas to bed. Things are not looking good.

So what do you do about it? Well, according to a recent study, nearly 50 percent of those age 35 to 65 decide to start their lives all over again. Some ditch jobs, houses, and marriages, while others seek fulfilment from extramarital affairs.

> **It's important to have a twinkle in your wrinkle.**
>
> —*Anonymous*

91

TRADING UP

Journalist Geoff Wolinetz has the, er, right idea: "I'm going to marry a girl that's kind of cute now but is guaranteed to either gain a lot of weight or lose her looks very quickly," he wrote for the *Yankee Pot Roast*. "This way, when I trade in for a much younger and much hotter girlfriend, my ex-wife will look even worse compared to her. If you want to have a decent midlife crisis, you really have to trade up."

Comedy writer Robert Orben evidently agrees. "I may be forty," he once said, "but every morning when I get up, I feel like a twenty-year-old. Unfortunately, there's never one around."

MY WIFE *DOES* UNDERSTAND ME

After 25 years of marriage, a man said to his wife, "Darling, twenty-five years ago we lived in a shabby apartment, drove a cheap car, slept on a pull-out bed, and watched a black-and-white portable TV. But every night, I got to sleep with a sexy twenty-five-year-old blonde. Now we have a dream house in the country, two nice cars, a king-size bed, and a plasma TV. But every night, I have to sleep with a fifty-year-old woman. It seems to me that life is not being very fair."

His wife, being a very reasonable sort of woman, told him to go out and find himself a nice, young, sexy 25-year-old blonde. She, in the meantime, would make sure he got the shabby apartment, cheap car, pull-out bed, and black-and-white portable TV back, too.

NOCTURNAL CREATURES

A recent survey was conducted to discover why men get out of bed in the middle of the night:

→ 5 percent said it was to get a glass of water.

→ 12 percent said it was to go to the bathroom.

→ 83 percent said it was to go home.

VIRTUAL ADULTERY

Forty-year-old David Pollard and his wife, Amy, who met on an Internet chat room, were avid fans of the Internet game Second Life, which allows players to create characters for themselves and to live in a virtual world complete with virtual jobs, homes, relationships, and children. David's Second Life character was called Dave Barmy, while Amy was DJ Laura Skye. The real-life couple married in the local town hall, while in a second—far more lavish—online wedding, their alter egos replicated the "fairy tale" ceremony of David and Victoria Beckham.

Alas, the Pollards' marriage was to be no fairy tale. A few months down the line, Amy woke from an afternoon nap to discover to her horror that her husband's online character was having sex with another female player.

"I caught him cuddling a woman on a sofa in the game," she said. "It looked really affectionate. I went crazy. I was so hurt. I just couldn't believe what he'd done. I looked at the computer screen and could see his character having sex with a female character. It's cheating, as far as I'm concerned."

Needless to say, Amy filed for divorce, claiming that David had committed adultery with the animated woman and that it was in fact the second time she had caught him cheating online.

Her attorney was not at all surprised. Apparently, it was the second divorce case involving Second Life that week.

THE PERFECT HUSBAND

A man wakes up one morning with the worst of hangovers and no memory whatsoever of the previous night. Slowly opening his eyes, he sees a packet of painkillers and a glass of water on the bedside table.

He looks around the room to find his clothes neatly folded on a chair with a clean, freshly ironed shirt on top. The bedroom is tidy, and on the pillow next to him is a note that says, "Sweetheart, your breakfast is in the kitchen. I love you."

Downstairs, he finds warm croissants, freshly squeezed orange juice, and a pot of coffee laid out on the table for him, along with his favorite newspaper. His teenage son is also there, getting ready for school.

"Tell me, son," asks the man, "what happened last night?"

"Well," says his son, "you came home so blind drunk you didn't even know your own name. You almost broke the door down, then you threw up all over the carpet in the hall, then you knocked the furniture over, and when Mom tried to calm you down, you thought she was the police, so you gave her a black eye."

"Good God!" says the man. "Then how come my clothes are all folded, the house is immaculate, and this breakfast has been laid out for me?"

"When Mom pushed you into the bedroom and tried to get your trousers off to put you into bed, you shouted, 'Get your hands off me, you filthy whore, I'm a married man!'"

When I die, I want it to be on my hundredth birthday, in my house on the beach in Maui, and my husband so upset that he has to drop out of college.

—*Roz*, Frasier

PRISONER OF LOVE

A woman wakes up in the middle of the night to find her husband missing from their bed. In the quietness of the house, she gradually makes out a muffled sound coming from downstairs.

She goes down and looks around but cannot find her husband. Listening carefully, she is sure she can hear the sound of moaning. She follows the sound down into the cellar and finds her husband huddled in a corner sobbing into the wall.

"What's wrong with you?" she asks.

"Remember when your father caught us together when you were sixteen?" he sobs. "And do you remember he said I had two choices: I could either marry you or spend the next twenty years in prison?"

"Yes, I remember," she says, puzzled. "So what?"

"I would have got out today."

> What most persons consider as virtue, after the age of 40 is simply a loss of energy.
>
> —*Voltaire*

THE ORIGINAL FREUDIAN SLIP

Legend has it that Sigmund Freud paid a visit to Carl Jung while on a trip to the United States.

Freud confided to Jung that, throughout his stay in the States, his sleep had been plagued with erotic dreams, which he suspected were caused by the provocative appearance of some of the American women. He told his friend, "I dream of prostitutes."

Jung, a shrink first and a friend second, thought Freud should try to psychoanalyze his way out of the problem and suggested, "Why don't you do something about it?"

Freud was indignant. "But I'm a married man!"

TIME TO SAY GOOD-BYE

A wife appears in court during her divorce trial. The judge quizzes her to establish the grounds for her divorce. She replies, "I'd like a cute little cottage on around three acres." The judge corrects himself, saying he was inquiring as to the nature of her relations with her husband.

"Well, my husband's parents live in the next town," she offers.

Growing a little exasperated now, the judge tries to simplify his question: "Do you have a grudge at all?" he asks her.

"Oh, yes," she responds, "with room for two cars and a spare refrigerator."

Fighting to contain his mounting irritation, the judge asks whether there has been any infidelity in the marriage.

"Not in the living room," the woman replies, "but our teenage sons both have CD players in their bedrooms."

The judge tries one last time: "Has your husband ever beaten you up?"

The woman smiles and says, "Yes, all the time; in fact, he's up first most mornings."

Throwing his hands up in despair, the judge cries, "Madam, why do you want this divorce?"

"Oh, I don't, Your Honor," she says. "It's my husband's fault. He says he's tired of not being able to communicate with me."

Instead of getting married again, I'm going to find a woman I don't like and just give her a house.

—Rod Stewart

A FRENCH AFFAIR

News of an extramarital affair at the White House would have the world's press in a frenzy for weeks. Not so in France, where the press celebrated 52-year-old president Nicolas Sarkozy's courtship of stunning supermodel-turned-rock-chick Carla Bruni.

Strictly speaking, the relationship wasn't adulterous: Sarkozy had recently gone through a quickie divorce. But he suffered from none of the coyness that would undoubtedly afflict other world leaders in a similar situation. In fact, he was happy to show off his 40-year-old trophy at every opportunity, posing for the photographers who snapped them strolling and kissing on an Egyptian beach, he in his presidential trunks, she in a tiny black bikini. Within a matter of a few short months, they were married.

For her part, Bruni is no retiring wallflower, either: Her previous high-profile affairs have split marriages and divided families. She was blamed for the divorce of Mick Jagger and Jerry Hall and caused a father-son rift between French publisher Jean-Paul Enthoven and his son Raphael, following romances with both men. Carla casts off her romantic track record with true panache, telling *Le Figaro Madame* magazine in February 2007, "I am a tamer [of men], a cat, an Italian—monogamy bores me terribly...I am faithful to myself!"

MANY HAPPY RETURNS

A middle-aged guy takes his wife out to dinner to celebrate her fortieth birthday.

"Well, my love," he asks, "what would you like for your birthday? A Jaguar? A fur coat? A diamond necklace?"

"Actually, darling," she answers. "What I really want is a divorce."

"Hell!" exclaims the husband. "I wasn't planning on spending that much."

> Why leave the nut you got for one
> you don't know?
>
> —*Loretta Lynin*, Esquire

You Feel the Need for Speed

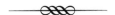

THE MEN-O-PORSCHE

That certain time in a man's life when the overwhelming need to buy a speedy motorcycle or a sleek, high-performance sports car coincides with the appearance of that first gray hair and the disappearance of a taut midriff. Along with the "mean machine" comes a wardrobe of trendy new clothes (all slightly too tight), an electric guitar, and an inappropriate new vocabulary borrowed from much younger colleagues.

A SENSIBLE SET OF WHEELS

So many men fall victim to a kind of vehicular madness when the midlife crisis hits them. In October 2002 Arnold Schwarzenegger seemed to prove he was a rare exception, taking the astonishing step of returning his newly bought Ferrari Spider to the dealership.

Fueled by political ambition but no doubt with heavy heart, Arnie explained that he had to think carefully about what his choice of car might say about him to potential voters. He told the dealer, "I feel I need a car that would better telegraph my image as a candidate for California governor. A car that says I'm a man of the people." Admirable decision.

Little more than six months later, Schwarzenegger could be seen proudly driving an Austrian tank around the streets of California.

STILL GOT WHAT IT TAKES?

If you find yourself worrying that your physical attractions are on the wane, that you're becoming invisible to the opposite sex and you are filled with an overwhelming urge to prove that you've still got it...well, then you know you've hit middle age full-on. But don't try to get yourself noticed in quite the same manner as the following examples of midlife madness.

A 34-year-old man from the historic town of Hradec Králové in the Czech Republic took middle-aged showing-off to the extreme when he drove a 12-ton armored personnel carrier through the streets of his hometown. Since only light vehicles are allowed in the historic center of town, the man was arrested and fined. His excuse? His car had broken down, it was too far to walk to the shops, and he had no choice but to use the gigantic fighting machine—bought from the Czech military—to go and buy ice cream for his demanding kids.

Alphons Edberg, a 33-year-old man from Hamburg, did what a lot of men at his age do: He went to a car dealership in search of the true meaning of life and took a Ferrari 360 Modena out for a test run. On seeing a beautiful woman walking along the road in front of him, Edberg decided to impress her with his admirable driving skills. Unfortunately, after putting his foot down, he lost control of the car and crashed into a tree, a road sign, and a fence before finally wrapping himself and the brand-new Ferrari around a lamppost.

ETERNAL YOUTHS

What is it with middle-aged men and motorcycles? Perhaps unsurprisingly, the average age of a Harley Davidson owner is 46. A 2004 article by Howard Jacobson in *The Independent* illustrated perfectly the chasm between appearance and reality when it comes to these middle-aged Hells Angels:

"Every Saturday afternoon, thirty or so bikers zoom up on gleaming machines, park very carefully and stride manfully into the Picasso [Café]. In their black leathers, gauntlets and body armour they are the last word in machismo. It's only when they remove their helmets that the myth explodes. They are all balding, bespectacled, middle-aged accountants…who make a great fuss about putting their helmets under the table so they won't get scratched."

MIDDLE-AGED BRAGGING

A man driving a Hyundai pulls up to a traffic light next to a Rolls-Royce. He looks the Rolls up and down admiringly and then opens his window and shouts, "Hey, nice car. Have you got a phone in that Rolls? I've got one in my Hyundai."

The Rolls-Royce driver looks at him in disdain and answers, "Of course I have a phone."

"Great!" says the driver. "Have you got a fridge, too? I've got one in the back of my Hyundai."

The driver of the Rolls, waiting impatiently for the lights to change, answers, "Yes, I have a fridge."

"Fantastic!" says the Hyundai driver. "What about a TV? I've got one of those in here, too!"

The Rolls driver, now very annoyed, says, "Yes, of course I have a TV! This is one of the most luxurious cars in the world, you know!"

"Well, that's super," says the Hyundai driver. "But what about a bed? Have you got a bed in there? I have a bed in the back of my Hyundai."

The lights change, and the Rolls driver, seething with rage at his own lack of a car bed, speeds away in a cloud of exhaust fumes. He drives straight to his dealership, where he orders a bed to be fitted into his car immediately. Pleased with the results, he drives around town until he spots the Hyundai parked at the side of the road with its windows all steamed up.

Getting out of his car, he knocks on the Hyundai's window and, when the driver pokes his head out, all soaking wet, announces proudly, "I now have a bed in my Rolls!"

The Hyundai driver looks at him incredulously and shakes his head. "You got me out of the shower to tell me *that?*"

> Here comes forty. I'm feeling my age and I've ordered the Ferrari. I'm going to get the whole midlife-crisis package.
>
> —*Keanu Reeves*

CARS AND WOMEN

One day God came down to Earth and said to three men, "The less you cheat on your wives, the bigger and better the cars you'll get in heaven."

The first man went to heaven after having cheated on his wife 67 times; he got a Mercedes. The second man went to heaven after having cheated on his wife twice; he got a Ferrari. When the third man got to heaven, he told God that he had never cheated on his wife, and his reward was a Bentley.

THE NEED FOR SPEED

One day the third man seemed strangely depressed, so his friends asked him what was wrong.

"I saw my wife the other day," he answered.

"Yes, so?" said his friends.

"She was riding a skateboard."

A FAIR COP

Paul had spent all his savings on a sleek Mercedes sports car and was out on the highway for an evening cruise. The top was down, the wind was blowing through his hair, and the needle was inching toward 100 M.P.H....and suddenly he saw a flashing blue light behind him.

There's no way they can catch me, Paul thought to himself, and put his foot down on the accelerator. By the time the speedometer touched 130, however, the blue lights were still flashing behind him.

What on earth am I doing? he thought, and pulled over. The officer came up to him, took his license, and examined it.

"Listen," said the officer. "I've had a tough shift, and this is my last pull-over. I don't feel like more paperwork, so if you can give me an original excuse for your crazy driving, you can go."

"Last week my wife ran off with a cop," said Paul, "and I was afraid you were trying to give her back."

"I see," said the officer. "Well, have a nice night."

YOU KNOW YOU'RE MIDDLE-AGED WHEN...
You're All a Twitter

Have you just tuned in to the social networking craze that has been sweeping the world up in its cyber arms? Facebook, Bebo, MySpace, Twitter…the list is endless. And it's not just for teenagers, either. If you're middle-aged, you're more likely to be at it than anybody else, it seems.

SOCIAL NETWORKING FOR "MIDDLESCENTS"

The only trouble is, while the teens of this world are using these sites to organize and shout about their fabulously drunken and outrageous social lives—inciting envy among their "friends"—many older Tweeters and Facebookers haven't quite got the hang of it yet, as the following examples of middle-aged celebrity twittering illustrate.

Check out my op-ed in *LA Times* on commonsense
reforms to eliminate fraud and waste to help
with the budget.
—*Arnold Schwarzenegger*

Mmmmmhmmmm. A nap and an orange.
I'm back in the game!
—*Pink*

Anybody got a surefire remedy for ticks?
Just pulled 8 off of 1 dog. None of the prescribed
vet meds seem to be working.
—*Oprah Winfrey*

In helsinki eating carrots. I know, the party
never stops (or starts, really).
—*Moby*

Just had delicious lunch with family cooked by
lovely wife. Have realized that while I adore pepper,
I find salt quite uninteresting.
—*Jonathan Ross*

Just emerged from dentist. Cracked molar. Bah.
—*Stephen Fry*

FIVE SIGNS YOU'RE ACTING LIKE
A MIDDLE-AGED FACEBOOKER

1. You can't wait to sign in each day, and you get overly excited when you receive a friend request. Unfortunately, it's usually a case of mistaken identity.

2. You overuse pointless applications, spending an inordinate amount of time throwing vampires, tungsten screws, sheep, cupcakes, pregnant teenagers, and an awful lot of hugs to people you haven't set eyes on for over 20 years.

3. Your profile picture is a photo of your child, and your albums have titles such as "First bath!" and "First tooth!!!!"

4. Your status updates tend to go along the lines of "Maria is doing her tax return" or "Paul is peeling potatoes."

5. You have eight friends, of which three are colleagues, one is your other half, and the rest are borrowed from your kids.

QUIZ: WHAT YOUR FACEBOOK GROUPS SAY ABOUT YOUR AGE

The habits of Facebookers who are at either end of the age spectrum are vastly different. Between them lies a murky melee of midlifers treading the precarious middle ground between vibrant youth and the slow, inevitable decline to Past-It Ville. Take this little quiz and let the results steer you into a wiser use of cyber networking:

1. You want a group that says, "I have my finger on the pulse of popular culture." Do you opt for:

a) AFTER HARRY POTTER SEVEN COMES OUT, ☐
I WON'T HAVE ANYTHING TO LIVE FOR

b) ELLEN DEGENERES FOR PRESIDENT ☐

c) IF JESUS HAD AN IPOD, THE BEATLES ☐
WOULD BE ON IT

d) ADDICTED TO SCRAPBOOKING? ☐
YOU'RE NOT ALONE

2. You want a cause that flags you up as someone with a social conscience. Do you join:

a) I WISH I COULD GIVE ALL MY FAT TO CHILDREN IN AFRICA ☐

b) BACK OFF JAPAN—LEAVE WHALES ALONE! ☐

c) OMG! I SO NEED A GLASS OF WINE OR I'M GOING TO SELL MY KIDS ☐

d) I BET I CAN FIND 1,000,000 PEOPLE WHO JUST WANT PEACE ☐

3. You're a political animal and you want the world to know it. Which group boasts the political platform you're most likely to be drawn to?

a) IF THIS GROUP GETS 1,000,000 MEMBERS, THE PRICE OF MARS BARS WILL HALVE ☐

b) PETITION TO GET MCDONALD'S TO DO DELIVERIES ☐

c) HELP MAKE GAS PRICES GO DOWN ☐

d) BRING BACK PROHIBITION ☐

4. You're at a crossroads in your life, a time of turbulent change. As those around you lunge into their own uncertain futures, you want a group that will give you time to reflect on who and where you are. You choose:

a) I MISS NAP TIME & RECESS ☐

b) MY FRIENDS ARE GETTING MARRIED, ☐
   I'M JUST GETTING DRUNK

c) THE ONLY BOSS I LISTEN TO IS BRUCE ☐
   SPRINGSTEEN

d) WHEN I WAS YOUR AGE, PLUTO WAS ☐
   A PLANET

5. You've lived life. Seen things the rest of us couldn't even imagine. You want a group that gets to the heart of your personal truth. You join:

a) WHATEVER I DID WHEN I WAS DRUNK ☐
   DIDN'T HAPPEN IF I DON'T REMEMBER IT

b) IN RETROSPECT, THAT WAS A POOR ☐
   CHOICE

c) JANE AUSTEN GAVE ME UNREALISTIC ☐
   EXPECTATIONS OF LOVE

d) A CUP OF TEA SOLVES EVERYTHING ☐

6. You are nothing if not brutally self-aware. To further your personal development, you feel the time is right for a public declaration of your greatest weakness. Is it more likely to be:

a) I LOVE IT WHEN PEOPLE I HATE GET FAT ☐

b) WRITING PAPERS SINGLE-SPACED FIRST MAKES MY DOUBLE-SPACED RESULT CLIMACTIC ☐

c) I JUDGE YOU WHEN YOU USE POOR GRAMMAR ☐

d) I'M INTELLECTUALLY PROMISCUOUS ☐

7. There's nothing wrong with your work ethic, but everyone needs to kick back now and again, right? So, once in a while, if you're honest with yourself, you cut corners. Face up to the Facebook group that best expresses your inner self:

a) I WISH MY WORK WOULD DO ITSELF ☐

b) I WISH MEETINGS HAD "AUTO-SUMMARIZE" ☐

c) I END UP ON FACEBOOK EVERY TIME I'M ON THE COMPUTER ☐

d) I LOVE NAPS ☐

8. You're a deeply spiritual being. Life for you is all about reflection and meditation. For kicks you like to indulge in some stimulation of the philosophical kind. The Facebook group that best caters to the contemplative mystic in you is:

a) BEER VS. VAGINA: THE ENDLESS DEBATE ☐

b) WAS JOSEF FRITZL A GOOD BUILDER? ☐

c) FORMULA 1, THE RELIGION ☐

d) FACEBOOK IS AN EVIL POSTMODERN ☐
   CONSTRUCTION RELEGATING LIFE TO
   A VIDEO GAME

9. You know what? Age is irrelevant. You have a young spirit—you're wild, you're impulsive. You just don't care! You join:

a) HONESTLY, I WRITE "LOL" AND I'M NOT ☐
   EVEN LAUGHING

b) I WEAR MY SUNGLASSES AT NIGHT ☐
   BECAUSE THE SUN NEVER SETS ON
   BEING BADASS

c) AUTOMATIC DOORS MAKE ME FEEL ☐
   LIKE A JEDI

d) IF HOT CHOCOLATE COULD GET ME ☐
   DRUNK, I'D BE AN ALCOHOLIC

10. Life is a nonstop intellectual roller coaster; a 3D technicolor spelling bee. You can't fight the urge to share your love of learning a moment longer. The group that offers you the best opportunity to make your own positive affirmation is:

a) ANYTHING WORTH LEARNING I LEARNED ☐ FROM "BEVERLY HILLS 90210"

b) THE ABILITY TO BULLSHIT IS AN ESSENTIAL ☐ LIFE SKILL

c) I WISH I WERE A DERIVATIVE SO I COULD ☐ LIE TANGENT TO YOUR CURVES

d) MY HATERS ARE MY MOTIVATORS ☐

THE RESULTS

Mostly A's

You're not so much youthful as a perpetual fresher. You snicker in the face of middle age and sashay through your midlife crisis. The only wisdom you've stored up along the way is the kind you've read on other people's tattoos, and you dip your toe in political and social causes in a vain attempt to show the world your thinking side. In truth, you're about as deep as a Britney Spears song lyric.

Mostly B's

You might pay lip service to being a grown-up by day, but you work hard during your downtime to perpetuate your image as the quirky embodiment of the whole "40 is the new 30" zeitgeist. Don't kid yourself that this is all good: Peter Pan doesn't look too hot with a paunch and slippers. So lose the teen speak and take on a responsibility or two before you forget how.

Mostly C's

Bingo! You embrace your age with gusto and creativity. You are at ease with yourself, flaws and all. You have the confidence to declare your cultural allegiances, even if they're not always cool. Your days of trying to be someone you're not are pretty much over, and life is generally sweet.

Mostly D's

Hey, Granddad, you're on dangerous territory. Your life has become one long round of nature documentaries and Sudoku. If that's what floats your boat, then fine; carry on. But once in a while, throw off your moccasins and take a risk or two while you can still haul yourself off the couch.

MINISTER OF MIDDLE-AGED INDISCRETIONS

A Uruguayan government minister got into hot water when she posted a naked picture of herself on Facebook. Daisy Tourné, Minister of the Interior, captioned the picture "There's nothing more natural than a woman in the shower."

Government opposition leaders were horrified at the exposure and labeled Tourné an exhibitionist whose "actions were unacceptable, particularly as she had responsibility for the police."

"I think it's in very bad taste that the minister exposes herself so intimately. Ministers have to be more austere, modest," former vice president Luis Hierro Lopez was quoted as saying.

But Daisy was unrepentant, claiming that the picture was taken in a shower used to rinse sand off after a visit to the beach and was never meant to be erotic or made available to the public. Fair enough, but that does beg the question, Why post it in the first place?

ENOUGH IS ENOUGH

For a lot of us middle-aged social networkers, Facebook, Twitter and others provided a whirlwind of 21st-century entertainment for the first two weeks of membership, at the end of which we sat back and asked ourselves what on earth we were doing messing around on sites designed for children.

Blogger Jellio, writing on the excellent pop-culture site www.yesbutnobutyes.com, couldn't agree more: "I've been poked, pinched, kissed, kicked, slapped and smooched. I've been bitten by vampires, mauled by werewolves and stabbed by pirates. I know my stripper, pimp and porn star names. And I've got fifty thousand dollars worth of fake money in the poker room. Can someone please tell me what the **** I'm doing. I'm forty for Pete's sake."

You Begin Behaving Badly

In generations past it was assumed that by the time you'd hit your thirties, you would be all grown up, could assume the mantle of respectable adulthood, and be ready to take on board all that being middle-aged and responsible entailed.

Not anymore, it seems, with the so-called "graying groovers"—people from their late twenties to their early forties—clinging to the remnants of their youth and refusing to behave in an age-appropriate manner. These "middle youths" may have a house in suburbia, a demanding job, a couple of kids, and a lawn to mow, but they can also be found gyrating in night clubs and lurching drunkenly in bars on a Friday night.

TEACHER TRAUMA

Becoming middle-aged doesn't necessarily guarantee good behavior. Not even if you've chosen to enter the respectable profession of teaching.

Pupils from a school in eastern Pennsylvania were shocked and bemused when their balding and bespectacled teacher decided to try out a new method of instilling discipline. When the 13- to 14-year-olds became unruly, the middle-aged man threatened to strip off his shirt and make them look at his untoned physique and man boobs as punishment.

The threat, far from silencing the pupils, only prompted them to goad him on. So, true to his word, he stripped off his shirt and exposed his love handles to the class.

Unfortunately, one fast-thinking pupil managed to capture the unexpected striptease on his cell phone and posted the film on a video-sharing website. Needless to say, the hapless teacher has since been banned from the classroom.

A VERY MERRY BISHOP

When the Bishop of Southwark Cathedral in London turned up to deliver his weekly sermon with a black eye and a bump on his head, he explained to his congregation that he had been mugged and had his briefcase, cell phone, and crucifix stolen. With his head too swollen to accommodate his miter, he also claimed to have little recollection of the incident.

The truth of the matter, as revealed by slightly more lucid witnesses, was of an entirely different nature. The bishop, it was said, had been drinking Portuguese wine at an Irish embassy reception and had left at around 9:00 P.M. to go home. At 9:30 he stumbled into a quiet street next to some railroad arches, where he climbed into a stranger's unattended car and began throwing toys out onto the road. The owner of the car—alerted by the vehicle's alarm—ran out into the street to confront the bishop, who was by now sitting in the backseat still dressed in his robes. Asked what he was doing in the car, the bishop replied, "I am the Bishop of Southwark; it's what I do."

The bishop had to be forcibly dragged from the car and fell onto the pavement during the scuffle. After refusing offers of help, he staggered into a railroad arch.

Luckily, his forgiving parishioners did not lose faith in him, with one stating, "Having a couple of drinks is not a sin; maybe he did not realize how strong the wine was."

SOUNDS LIKE TROUBLE

While we would like to think that behind the old saying "With age comes wisdom" there is at least a hint of truth, unfortunately for many midlifers this isn't the case at all. Grasping at the last vestiges of a rebellious youth can only spell trouble—and it's no longer your dad bellowing up the stairs for you to turn the music down.

Thirty-year-old Teresa Webb found this out the hard way when she insisted on playing her favorite song, Peter Kay's "Is This the Way to Amarillo?," at full volume. Indeed, she played the song so loudly and so frequently that she was issued with a noise-abatement order. Still undeterred, Teresa continued to blast out her favorite lyrics, forcing one of her neighbors to sell her house and move.

She was eventually taken to court, where her stereo was seized, she was given a two-year Anti-Social Behavior Order, and warned she could be jailed for five years if she was caught playing loud music again.

Wow. Dad was never *that* strict!

> They keep sending me stuff
> for mothers of stroppy teenagers.
> But *I'm* still a stroppy teenager.
>
> —*Madonna*

WEIGHT-WATCHERS

Even trying to hold back the onset of the middle-age spread can get you into hot water with the law, as 36-year-old bodybuilder Giran Jobe soon discovered when his neighbors began complaining about his overly exuberant exercise routines.

His two-hour training sessions, complete with grunting and the sound of his dumbbells being thrown to the floor, were so loud that they reached the same level of decibels as a rock concert. After repeated warnings from the town to ditch the weights, Jobe was eventually fined $115. He promised to forgo the weightlifting in favor of some peaceful push-ups and sit-ups.

"I don't play loud music, I don't have parties and I don't stamp around," he lamented. "All I do is exercise and work out with my weights. I am trying to keep fit. I cannot believe I got taken to court for exercising."

LAWN MAINTENANCE

A middle-aged man from Wisconsin found the pressure of keeping his lawn trim too overwhelming. After repeatedly trying to start up his lawn mower without success, he lost his temper and fired at the offending machine with a shotgun.

He was promptly arrested for disorderly conduct and for possession of a short-barreled shotgun or rifle. To make matters worse, he was told it was unlikely the lawn mower could ever be repaired. A bad day all around!

> When we remember we are all mad, the mysteries disappear and life stands explained.
>
> —*Mark Twain*

YOU KNOW YOU'RE MIDDLE-AGED WHEN...

You Say and Do the Dumbest Things

Do you sometimes worry that the wisdom we are supposed to enjoy with age is somehow passing you by? Are you plagued by the conviction that you are growing a little dumber with every advancing year?

If so, it may not all be in your imagination. A recent study reported an unnerving medical phenomenon that might account for your declining mental agility: Twenty years of research indicated that people who went on to develop heart disease in later life had demonstrated deteriorating cognitive abilities in middle age. In other words, they experienced a midlife dumbing down.

For those of us swayed by science, all this is sobering stuff. But don't just take the nerds' word for it; check out this priceless selection of encyclopedic wisdom from some of the world's most prominent middle-aged celebs, and draw your own conclusions....

They're causing me to say very mumbly-jumbly
things on [*American*] *Idol.*
—*Paula Abdul*

I dress sexily—but not in an obvious way.
Sexy in a virginal way.
—*Victoria Beckham*

And now the sequence of events in no particular order.
—*Dan Rather*

The word "genius" isn't applicable in football.
A genius is a guy like Norman Einstein.
—*Joe Theisman*

Ice is very much like flowers. It just dies at a certain
point. But you know what's weird? You can bring it back
to life. Just by freezing it. Ice, I worship it.
—*Drew Barrymore*

You can expect Bobby to be Bobby. If Bobby ain't Bobby,
then Bobby just can't be Bobby.
—*Bobby Brown*

The man for me is now the cherry on the pie,
but I'm the pie and my pie is good all by itself,
even if I don't have a cherry.
—*Halle Berry*

If I was a giraffe, and someone said I was a snake,
I'd think, no, actually I'm a giraffe.
—*Richard Gere*

I was in a no-win situation, so I'm glad that
I won rather than lost.
—*Frank Bruno*

The only happy artist is a dead artist, because only
then you can't change. After I die, I'll probably
come back as a paintbrush.
—*Sylvester Stallone*

Changing someone's life is not the best, is not wanting
to change the other life. It is being who you are that
changes another's life. Do you understand?
—*Juliette Binoche*

I feel my best when I'm happy.
—*Winona Ryder*

If you have intercourse you run the risk of dying,
and the ramifications of death are final.
—*Cyndi Lauper*

It's really hard to maintain a one-on-one relationship if
the other person is not going to allow me
to be with other people.
—*Axl Rose*

Researchers have discovered that chocolate produces
some of the same reactions in the brain as marijuana.
The researchers also discovered other similarities between
the two, but can't remember what they are.
—*Matt Lauer*

HIGH-SPEED CAT-AND-MOUSE

Getting caught acting dumb is never a good thing. Getting caught acting dumb with a pistol in your pocket is a terrible thing.

In July 2008 a 43-year-old Californian woman was traveling at top speed through Potter Valley when she spotted a mouse scurrying across the floor of the car. But her quick-draw reactions were to backfire, literally. Pulling a .44-caliber Magnum from its holster, she fired at the creature, accidentally dropping the gun as she did so. The bullet ricocheted off the floor, sliced through the woman's knee and through her male companion's pants, grazing his groin and coming to a rest in his pocket.

The mouse was not hurt.

AWARD-WINNING BLUNDER

During the live broadcast of MTV's 2002 Video Music Awards, Britney Spears invited Michael Jackson up on stage to receive a cake in celebration of his forty-fourth birthday. As he was making his way to the front, Britney commented that, in her opinion, Michael was the artist of the millennium.

Jackson, evidently overcome with an inflated sense of occasion, took the mic and declared, "When I was a little boy growing up in Indiana, if someone told me I'd be getting the Artist of the Millennium award, I'd never have believed it!"

A shame-faced MTV spokesperson later assured the press that there was, in fact, no such award as Artist of the Millennium.

A DUMB EYE-DEA

It's not just people in the public eye who commit acts of random midlife stupidity.

In October 2008, police in Sweden pulled over a car being driven erratically by a 56-year-old woman. When her blood-alcohol levels turned out to be almost 10 times the legal limit, the woman pleaded for leniency. She insisted her driving had not been hazardous; she had simply taken the precaution of driving with one eye closed so as to avoid seeing double.

> You are only young once, but you can be immature for a lifetime.
>
> —John P. Grier

TOTALLY LOCO

Three middle-aged guys decide to spend a day hunting. The first man sets off in search of a rabbit and returns a while later carrying a rabbit. Amazed, the others ask for the secret of his success.

"Simple," he says. "I saw tracks. I followed the tracks. I got me a rabbit."

So the second guy sets off in search of a deer and returns 20 minutes later hauling a deer corpse behind him. His friends are impressed and ask how he did it. Drawing himself up tall, he replies, "I saw tracks. I followed the tracks. I got me a deer."

So the last guy, buoyed by his friends' hunting successes, announces, "I'm just gonna shoot at whatever comes along."

The sun is setting by the time he drags himself back to his friends. He's battered, bruised, and bloodied, and collapses, exhausted, beside the two men. Anxiously, they ask him what happened.

"I saw tracks. I followed the tracks. I got hit by a train!"

OBEDIENT BUT DIM

Those navigation systems can be frustrating things. They have an authoritative insistence that makes it very difficult to disobey their instructions, even if you want to.

A 43-year-old German motorist found it impossible not to carry out his nav's directions to the letter. When the disembodied voice commanded him to "Turn right now," he did just that, veering off the road through a building site and up a stairway before finally crashing into a portable toilet and coming to a halt.

A MIDLIFE MAKEOVER

A middle-aged woman walked into her kitchen one Sunday morning and was encouraged to find her normally DIY-shy husband painting the walls.

Puzzled, she asked why he was wearing a denim jacket as well as a thick wool coat.

Exasperated, her husband pointed to the instructions on the paint tin: "For best results, apply two coats."

LIKE FATHER, LIKE SON

A middle-aged couple with two stunningly beautiful teenage daughters decided to try one last time for the son they had always wanted.

After months of trying, the wife finally became pregnant and, sure enough, delivered a healthy baby boy nine months later. The joyful father rushed into the nursery to see his new son and was horrified to see the ugliest child he had ever laid eyes on. He went to his wife and told her there was no way he could be the father of such a hideous baby.

"Look at the two beautiful daughters I fathered!" he cried. "It's obvious you've been cheating on me."

The wife just smiled sweetly at his bulbous nose and bulging eyes and said, "Not this time."

It's Time for Something Different

A face-lift, a mistress, a body piercing, an extreme sport…the midlife crisis leaves very few of us untouched. Frighteningly, it is now manifesting itself in men and women from as early as their twenties.

With no two MLCs the same, you can never predict the bizarre and mysterious ways in which you might find yourself affected.

SPACED OUT

A 43-year-old female astronaut from Houston certainly experienced a midlife crisis with a difference when she became the first active astronaut in history to face a felony charge.

Although married with three children, Lisa Nowak found herself falling—in typical middle-aged fashion—for

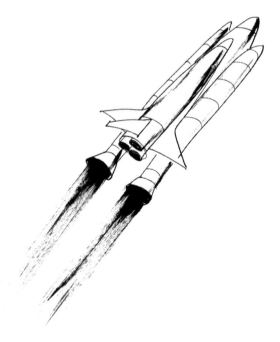

fellow astronaut William Oefelein. But she also believed she had a rival for his affections in the shape of Air Force engineer Colleen Shipman, and she took drastic measures to deal with the situation.

Hearing that her rival was due to land at Orlando one morning, Nowak drove 900 miles from Houston—reportedly wearing an adult diaper to avoid having to stop during the journey—in order to confront her. Dressed in a wig and a trench coat, Nowak approached her love rival in the airport car park and sprayed her in the face with pepper spray before making a quick getaway.

She was arrested soon after, and police were surprised to find in her possession a steel mallet, a BB gun, a knife, plastic bags, and several feet of rubber tubing. Nowak was charged with attempted murder after failing to convince police that the incriminating items were only intended to scare her rival.

BREAST IS BEST

While most men are content to stick with having a more traditional midlife crisis, Stu Rasmussen from Silverton, Oregon, chose an altogether more unusual way to deal with his.

During his second term as the mayor of Silverton, Rasmussen confessed to having been a cross-dresser all his life. He subsequently swapped his shirt and tie for high heels and a pair of breasts when he was elected mayor for the third time, becoming the first-ever openly transgender mayor in the United States.

"Some guys' midlife crisis is motorcycles or sports cars or climbing mountains or trophy wives or whatever," said Rasmussen. "My midlife crisis was quite different. I always wanted cleavage, so I went out and acquired some."

MIDLIFE THE MASAI WAY

Pity the male of Kenya and Tanzania's Masai culture: He has his midlife crisis thrust upon him and then marked by a public ceremony!

As a young man, a Masai warrior is known as a Moran. He carries a spear to defend his village from attack and is allowed to wear his hair long. Once he reaches his twenties, however, he is deemed to be middle-aged and ready to join the elders of the society via a transitional ceremony known as the Eunoto.

The rituals of the ceremony take place in a hut built specifically for the occasion; the warrior must drink blood from a freshly slaughtered bullock's neck and then have his long hair shaved off by his mother while sitting on the same cowhide on which he was circumcised years earlier. He is then permitted to select any woman he wants for his wife and is officially declared an elder.

TAKING THE SCENIC ROUTE

As we reach middle age and inevitably begin to take stock of our lives and careers, we may well fantasize about the glamorous lifestyles of Hollywood stars, wishing we could experience their immense wealth and easy lives. But what about middle-aged Hollywood celebrities? What do they do to take time out from the day-to-day stresses of life in the public eye?

Trainspotting and *Moulin Rouge!* star Ewan McGregor was able to do something totally out of the ordinary when, at age 33, he and his 37-year-old friend Charley Boorman took off on motorcycles to ride from London to New York—the long way around.

The 2004 trip, which covered 19,000 miles and took three and a half months, was an exhilarating experience for McGregor and Boorman but was not without its share of accidents and other near disasters. From obstructive border guards to dangerously fast rivers and from badly damaged motorcycles to particularly vicious mosquitoes, the two men might have been forgiven for admitting defeat and going home. But when they finally rode into New York screaming "We did it!" at the top of their lungs, it was clear that this particular midlife stunt was a conquest rather than a crisis.

TIME OUT FROM THE WORLD

A considerably less public way to celebrate the coming of middle age is to take yourself off to some quiet corner of the Earth and set up home there.

That is precisely what journalist Geraint Jones did in 2007. Browsing the Internet one day, he saw four acres for sale in the Chilterns, in southern England, and decided that it was just the middle-aged escape he was looking for.

Writing in the *Daily Mail*, Jones recalled his delight at leaving behind the stress and smog of London to set up a makeshift home among the trees. He even hosted a dinner party for friends, serving up lamb stew cooked over an open fire.

The only real problem was the reaction of his family to this newfound love of the Robin Hood lifestyle. While his partner showed some willingness by visiting twice, briefly, his son had to be bribed with promises of a trip to the local pub. But Jones is undeterred.

"As midlife crises go," he wrote, "this is surely more socially acceptable than acquiring a mistress or a Harley Davidson motorcycle."

JOHN TRAVOLTA'S MIDLIFE WANDERLUST

Whenever Hollywood legend John Travolta feels midlife is threatening his mojo, he hops into one of his private jets and heads off for a midlife crisis–busting adventure.

"I have a wanderlust for adventure," he says. "I will go off at any moment with the family and friends to explore the world. I go around the world once a year to Africa or Russia, and I love it. That keeps any midlife crisis at bay. I'm too blessed to be stressed."

BUT I DON'T OWN A PRIVATE JET

If, like Travolta, you're bored by the prospect of keeping your weight down and your spirits up with hours at the gym—and if you don't happen to have a fleet of jets sitting around in the garage—why not spice up your life with a midlife challenge of global proportions such as these?

→ Glacial abseiling in Alaska

→ Cycling the world's highest road across the Ladakh plateau in India, including a killer 26-mile uphill push

→ Braving the polar bears on a cross-country ski to the North Pole

→ Zipwiring across the treetops of the Colombian rain forests

→ Running the Marathon des Sables, the equivalent of six regular marathons, through the blistering heat of the Sahara Desert

WAVING AWAY THE MIDLIFE CRISIS

Celebrity chef Gordon Ramsay took up surfing during his midlife crisis, finding the exhilaration of the waves the perfect antidote to turning 40. Unfortunately, he discovered that looking professional *and* sexy while surfing wasn't quite as easy as younger experts made it look.

"Trying to get a fifteen-stone beached whale on a board while not looking like an idiot is not easy," he lamented to the *Daily Star*.

He did, however, suggest that wearing a wetsuit two sizes too small helped him look particularly attractive to any celeb-spotting onlookers.

> Boys will be boys, and so will a lot of middle-aged men.
>
> —*Kin Hubbard*

AND NOW FOR SOMETHING
COMPLETELY DIFFERENT

When writer Geoff Wolinetz decided it was high time for a midlife crisis–inspired change of lifestyle, he was determined not to do it by halves.

Writing for the *Yankee Pot Roast*, Wolinetz declared that "any sport where the pants are plaid and the shirt requires a collar is automatically out," and he announced that one particular "sport" seemed particularly perfect for an original midlife crisis: bear-baiting.

"They release you into this wildlife preserve with a side of beef and a small knife," he explained, probably not assuaging the fears of any readers, "and you engage in hand-to-hand combat with a ferocious grizzly bear. It's young, edgy and f----- crazy."

We can't argue with that.

> It's a sobering thought: When Mozart was my age, he had been dead for two years.
>
> —*Tom Lehrer, 37*

YOU KNOW YOU'RE MIDDLE-AGED WHEN…
Your Sport Turns Extreme

Sooner or later most of us have a wake-up call: the moment when something happens to make us finally accept that we're not the Action Man or the It Girl we once were. For some, it's the moment the office hottie walks into the room and you realize you didn't even bother pulling in your stomach. For others, it's the first time someone phones at 9:00 P.M. and says, "Sorry, did I wake you?"

Yup, the waist line's expanding, the hair's thinning, and everything else is either slowing down, seizing up, or heading south. But fear not! Life need not get in the way of adventure if you follow the lead of these middle-aged extreme-sports enthusiasts.

A FIENNES IDEA

After a career in the British Army and its elite special-forces unit, the SAS, a middle-aged man might be expected to put his feet up and enjoy life's more relaxing pursuits.

Sir Ranulph Fiennes, a cousin of Hollywood stars Ralph and Joseph, evidently thinks differently. He turned to adventuring after leaving the army and has conquered the world's highest peaks and most isolated places.

Not deterred by near-death experiences at the North and South poles—nor by a heart attack and the loss of his left fingers due to severe frostbite—Fiennes took on a new challenge in 2003, in his late fifties. He announced that he would complete seven marathons on seven continents in only seven days.

Following a grueling series of races in Patagonia, the Falkland Islands, Sydney, Singapore, London, and Cairo, Fiennes made it to New York, where he completed his challenge and announced that he would never do anything like that again.

He has since climbed the North Face of the Eiger and reached the summit of Mount Everest.

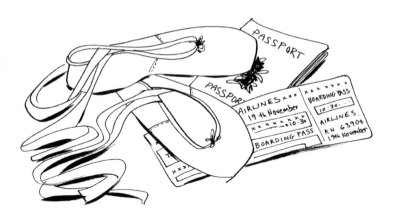

IN-FLIGHT ENTERTAINMENT

For the busy midlifer, finding time in a packed schedule for exercise isn't always easy. The svelte and toned *Kill Bill* actress, Uma Thurman, is living proof that busy is no excuse: Where there's a will, there's a way. She utilized her downtime onboard a flight from New York to Salt Lake City in 2009 by vacating her seat and using the aisle space as a ballet barre, doing yoga stretches and ballet moves for a full 20 minutes to the bemusement of her fellow passengers.

> ### Pushing 50 is exercise enough.
>
> *—Anonymous*

MOUNTAIN UNICYCLING

When Orange County piano tuner Terry Peterson turned 50 and discovered he could no longer button up his jeans, he decided to do something about it. Rejecting the usual dull, easy options, Terry resurrected a favorite hobby of his youth: unicycling. But cycling on a flat surface didn't give Terry the adrenaline hit he craved. He was looking for something more hard core and less clownish.

So Terry took his passion for life on one wheel to the mountain and now clocks up a staggering 60 hours a week mountain unicycling. Cycling uphill and down on a one-wheeled bike with no gears and no brake is quite a skill, but Terry takes it all in stride, telling the *Orange County Register*, "It's a lot like life.... I try not to avoid the obstacles. I like to confront them head-on and get over them."

> **You can't turn back the clock.**
> **But you can wind it up again.**
>
> —*Bonnie Prudden, rock climber*

FROM TANKS TO SKATEBOARDS

We all know that a male midlife meltdown is a common occurrence, but it looks as if even Action Man—the iconic action figure—has succumbed to the real-life stresses of middle age.

Following a youth spent as a respected military man who wore his khakis with pride and operated guns, tanks, and missiles with ease, fortysomething Action Man seems to have lost his way. Decked out in a selection of outfits

ranging from cycling shorts to jogging bottoms, he has ditched the tanks for sports cars and motorcycles and taken up a variety of extreme sports, including skydiving, windsurfing, climbing, and skateboarding.

But sales figures having taken a nosedive, and it seems the middle-aged doll's new lifestyle suggests he is struggling to keep up with his younger action-figure rivals. Sound familiar?

> You're never too old to become younger.
>
> —*Mae West*

FREE AS A BIRD

In 2004 Scottish comedian Billy Connolly embraced an opportunity to go bungee-jumping from a cable car high above a gorge in Queenstown, New Zealand. At the last moment, Billy was offered the opportunity to jump for free—as long as he agreed to do it butt naked.

"You get it for free if you do it naked," he told *The Age*. "So, being Scottish, I whipped the gear off and dived into the valley.... Besides, if you do it not naked, all the money can fly out of your pockets."

So, wearing nothing but his harness, Connolly leaped from the car, gleefully shouting, "Oh, yes! That'll do!" as he tumbled through the air. He later admitted that the experience leaves "two lumps in the back of your throat."

ROCKING AND ROLLING

Thirty-seven-year-old Billie Joe Armstrong, front man for rock band Green Day, finds release in sports when feeling the strain of a heavy tour schedule. But he's not interested in traditional middle-aged sports such as golf or squash: for Billie Joe, it's all about the skateboard.

"It keeps my mind off the music for a while," he told *Rolling Stone* magazine, boasting, "I've got a real Max Schaaf board."

Armstrong is fortunate in that his wife's brother is professional skateboarder Steve Nesser, a man who clearly has high ambitions for Billie Joe's skateboarding prowess.

"I've been skating a ramp," said Armstrong. "One of those half pipes that go from side to side."

For the time being, however, his hopes of pulling off some major four-wheeled magic are still little more than pipe dreams.

"I can roll back and forth," he confessed, "but that's it."

> **I do not participate in any sport with ambulances at the bottom of a hill.**
>
> —*Erma Bombeck*

You Turn into a Klutz

So how many times this week have you spilled your non-fat latte over your laptop? Sat on your reading glasses? Cut yourself shaving? Have you had a rash of spillages, breakages, and bruises? Do the days when you were lithe and nimble seem like a distant memory? Have you become a middle-aged klutz?

Fortunately, you're not alone. In fact, you're in some pretty good company....

STAGE FRIGHT

When presenting a *Kerrang!* rock music award to Marilyn Manson in 2000, former Bond girl Britt Ekland got up from her table to approach the stage but slipped on a mass of fruit, spilled drinks, and food littering the floor, following an earlier food fight between bad rockers Slip Knot and other bands.

Britt struggled onto the stage with the help of a burly security guard and presented the award. Despite being in pain, she even issued a good-hearted challenge to Slip Knot to try to upstage her, before being rushed to the hospital and treated for broken bones in her ankles and wrists.

As it turned out, Slip Knot had no trouble upstaging the glamorous Ekland: The group spent the evening breaking glasses and bottles and setting fire to their table.

HOLLYWOOD'S CLUMSIEST ACTOR

If you're clumsy, you're clumsy, and there's often nothing you can do but bring along your klutziness to work with you. Many Hollywood A-listers have notched up plenty of workplace accidents during their career.

Anthony Hopkins had to be treated for hypothermia after he slipped and fell into a Canadian river during the filming of *The Edge* in 1997. James Caviezel, the lead in *The Passion of Christ*, dislocated his shoulder before being struck by lightning while on the set. Even Nicole Kidman slipped and broke a rib during a dance routine, on the set of *Moulin Rouge!*

But queen of the celebrity klutz has to be actor Halle Berry, who has suffered such a long list of on-set accidents that she was voted Hollywood's Clumsiest Actor in 2003 by *In Touch* magazine. She has smashed her head against set lights, had smoke-grenade shrapnel removed from her eye, and broken her arm in fight scenes, while a car accident in 2000 left her with 22 stitches in her forehead. But even her love scenes have proved unexpectedly eventful, as Pierce Brosnan discovered when shooting a steamy bedroom scene for *Die Another Day*. The scene ended abruptly when Halle began gagging and waving her arms about wildly: She was choking on a piece of fruit.

> We don't stop playing because we grow old; we grow old because we stop playing.
>
> —*George Bernard Shaw*

WORKING YOURSELF INTO AN EARLY GRAVE

A middle-aged grave digger had a misfortunate workplace accident at a cemetery in Zwolle, Belgium. As he dug, he was loading the earth into a trailer perched alongside the grave. But he had parked the trailer on unstable ground, and after one shovelful too many, it tipped, emptying its contents into the grave in which the grave digger was standing. He was entirely buried and was saved only by his quick-thinking workmate, who was able to uncover his face until firefighters arrived to free him.

THE CLUMSY COOK

Oscar-winning actress Kate Winslet may have it all going on in front of the camera, but she is the first to admit that she's a klutz in the kitchen, particularly when preparing the most stressful meal of the year: Christmas dinner. Appearing on *The Late Show with David Letterman*, she showed off a frightening array of cookery scars.

"This was a really nasty burn when I was pre-preparing Christmas things…I sliced off a piece of my finger and saw it fall onto the chopping board with a piece of nail still attached!…I burned myself on a plate as I was serving up the dinner, so then I sat and ate my Christmas meal with my hand in a bowl of ice on my lap."

Letterman responded, "'So maybe cooking is not for you….'"

BAD-LUCK MASCOT

A man had spent months in a coma. Throughout the long, lonely days and nights, his wife had remained steadfastly at his bedside, keeping vigil. Finally, her husband came to. The woman was overjoyed and inched closer to his face to hear what he had to say.

"Honey," he whispered tearfully, "you have stayed with me come what may. I lost my job; you were at my side. My business failed; you stuck by me. I was run over by a bus; you were right there. I got sick; you never left my bedside." His wife was overcome with emotion and leaned in closer.

"You know what?" he continued. "I think you're bad luck."

THE WORLD'S LUCKIEST KLUTZ?

Some of the most spectacularly accident-prone midlifers can't always be accused of clumsiness. No matter how cool, calm, and collected they are, bad luck seems to seek some people out. Take John Lyne, for example, whose story was reported in the *Mirror* in 2006.

John's life has become a litany of life-threatening accidents. His terrifying workplace upsets have included a near collision with a large bucket of stone dropped by a colleague in a tunnel they were digging. Over the course of his career, he has also had ladders collapse under him while working on a roof and has fallen through an open inspection hatch. He's broken ribs, injured his back, and damaged limbs, but has somehow managed to escape with his life every time.

Over the years, John has also found little safety in his leisure time. He was once hit by a double-decker bus while out shopping, and he struck an electric cable during an over enthusiastic DIY session at home. The bad luck has even followed him on vacation: One year his cabdriver in Greece fell asleep at the wheel on his way back to the airport; the following year, his plane was struck by lightning soon after takeoff.

Is John plain unlucky, or is he a fortunate klutz with nine lives?

> I was thinking about how people seem to read the Bible a whole lot more as they get older. Then it dawned on me . . . they're cramming for their final exam.
>
> —George Carlin

COFFEE BREAK-IN

A middle-aged man from Kansas ran into a convenience store and demanded all the money in the cash drawer. Unfortunately, the cash drawer was mostly empty, so the crook decided instead to tie up the clerk and work the counter himself.

Three hours later he was arrested by two police officers who noticed the clerk tied up in the back room. But it was only after the crook had poured them two cups of coffee.

ONE-WAY STREET TO MIDDLE AGE

Stressed at work, harassed by young kids, and generally feeling the early pangs of a midlife crisis, Carol decided to go for a long, relaxing drive. As she headed onto the expressway, she turned on the radio and heard her favorite song and gradually felts her worries drifting away.

Suddenly the song was interrupted by an urgent radio announcement: "Attention all drivers on the left lane of the expressway: There is a dangerous driver traveling toward you in the wrong direction! I repeat, a dangerous driver traveling in the wrong direction on the expressway!" One? thought Carol, swerving to avoid yet another oncoming car, there are absolutely hundreds of them!

Your Wisdom Saves the Day

You just have to take a look at the rising number of middle-aged superheroes on the big screen in recent years to see that there's no upper age limit on heroic behavior. From Will Smith as Hancock to Halle Berry as Storm in *X-Men*, it seems the future safety of our planet is very much in the hands of the middle-aged.

So why not stir things up a little in your own life with a few acts of random heroism?

THE ADULT TOY FOR A MIDLIFE SUPERHERO

Bosses of the Japanese toy industry, struggling with the country's declining birth rate, have hit upon a stellar ploy to boost profits. They've begun marketing specifically designed toys to an entirely new demographic: middle-aged businessmen.

One product that has proved particularly popular is a gadget belt based on the one traditionally worn by 1970s Japanese superhero Kamen Rider. Many businessmen remember coveting this gadget-filled utility belt first time around and are delighted by the new, upgraded, fully grown-up leather version, with its flickering LED lights and extra roominess, designed with the middle-aged paunch in mind.

An official from Bandai, the company that produces the belt, explained, "When you grow up, you face lots of loathsome things in your workplace or at home. Once you put this belt on, however, you can be Kamen Rider the hero, or a different self."

BEYONCE AND WONDER WOMAN

With a constant parade of comic-book heroes making a big-screen comeback, the role of the female superhero is long overdue for a revamp. Ripe for a remake is lean Lynda Carter's 1970s phenomenon, *Wonder Woman*. And Beyoncé has her eye on the role.

Beyoncé told the *LA Times* in 2008 that having performed in a series of highly emotional roles has taken its toll. Now she's ready to pander to her inner superhero, "and what would be better than Wonder Woman? It would be great. And it would be a very bold choice. A black Wonder Woman would be a powerful thing. It's time for that, right?"

But the pressure of squeezing into that unforgiving little stars-and-stripes leotard is in the forefront of Beyoncé's mind.

"The way that Lynda Carter wore it, she was *so* fine. She was amazing.... Her waist was unbelievable. It was pretty crazy, actually, her proportions. But I love Wonder Woman, and it'd be a dream come true to be that character. It sure would be handy to have that lasso. To make everybody tell the truth? I need that."

REAL-LIFE CELEBRITY HEROES

When your working life all takes place on camera and involves you leaping into burning buildings, tackling endless bad guys, getting locked up in Bangkok prisons under false pretenses, and saving people's lives on a daily basis, sooner or later some of that machismo is bound to spill over into real life. Either that, or some of Hollywood's biggest names are just born heroes. Check out this list of real-life heroic celebrity midlifers:

Brad Pitt pulled a teenage fan from a lake after the boy fell in during an autograph-signing session on a boat at the Venice Film Festival in 2008.

Arnold Schwarzenegger starred in his very own real-life rescue scene in Hawaii, saving a guy who was drowning and bringing him back to shore on a boogie board.

Johnny Depp rescued a group of extras from certain injury on the set of *Public Enemies* in 2008. Six extras had their backs turned as a stunt car hurtled toward them after the driver lost control of the vehicle. Depp lunged at the group and flung them out of the car's path.

Renee Zellwegger paid no heed to her own safety after she saw a stranger collapse and slide unconscious down a steep canyon in California. She slid down to tend to the woman until help arrived.

Vin Diesel pulled an entire family out of an upturned burning vehicle after a car crash on a Hollywood freeway in 2002. Moments after he had pulled them free, the car was engulfed by flames.

Cuba Gooding, Jr. pulled up at a fast-food restaurant in Hollywood in 2007 to the sound of gunshots and the scene of a young man staggering and holding his head. Gooding got out of his car and tended to the wounded man, flagging down a passing police car and staying with the victim until ambulance crews arrived.

Jack Osbourne was taking a walk through London in 2008 when he saw a woman's bag being grabbed by a robber. Leaping immediately into action, Osbourne chased the thief and fought him to the ground and was able to restrain him until the police arrived.

REAL-LIFE WONDER WOMAN

If the thought of carrying out death-defying acts of heroism in your civvies just doesn't swing it for you, take inspiration from the story of New York City's Terrifica, a female masked avenger who patrols the city's clubs on her avowed mission to protect inebriated women from unscrupulous men.

Clad entirely in red, in the obligatory jumpsuit and cloak, and with the added precaution of a well-stocked utility belt—lipstick, pepper spray, cell phone, a journal, and candy for energy—Terrifica is convinced single girls need her protection.

"I do this because women are weak," she told the press. "They are easily manipulated, and they need to be protected from themselves and most certainly from men and their ill intentions toward them."

Heroic sentiments indeed. During daylight hours, however, like all truly great superheroes, Terrifica adopts a cunning disguise: She shrinks back into obscurity in the role of a 30-year-old office worker named Sarah, who, Terrifica notes with some scorn, "is a very weak woman. Very needy, insecure."

In turn, Sarah admits, "As soon as I pull on that mask, I feel really strong." The memory of having been dumped "in the most brutally humiliating of ways" is what led her into her original choice of freelance work.

FOR THE FINAL TIME, FACE IT!
You Know You're
Middle-Aged When...

1. You automatically receive help packing your groceries in the "10 items or less" lane.

2. You've found yourself discussing rain gutters and the merits of covering your boiler with insulation.

3. You totally buy into anti-wrinkle creams.

4. You've come to the irritating conclusion that your parents were right about everything after all.

5. You realize that you are now one of the geeky people walking around DisneyWorld wearing brightly colored shorts and a ridiculous hat.

6. Your weight-lifting routine has no effect on your muscles, but the veins on the backs of your hands are bulking up quite nicely.

7. You can pack two suits, seven shirts, three ties, seven pairs of pants, seven pairs of socks, a spare pair of shoes, and all your toiletries into a carry-on bag—in under three minutes.

8. A young lady offers you her seat on the train.

9. You wake up in a cold sweat during the night worrying that you haven't put the garbage out for collection.

10. You have to think for a second before addressing your kids so as to be sure to say the right name.

11. Over the weekend, when your wife mentions "some warm oil, a little friction, and a lot of squealing," you reassure her you'll take the car to be repaired first thing Monday morning.

12. You join a book group.

13. You start stories with, "When I was young…" and end them with, "You'll see—when you get to my age."

14. You've had at least three opportunities to buy every special-edition animated Disney movie "for the last time in a generation."

15. Wal-Mart now shares your fashion sense.

16. You find yourself strangely attracted to vegan shoes.

17. You develop a sudden obsession with the state of your teeth.

18. You decide it's high time you start writing that novel you've been going on about for the past fifteen years.

19. You start saying things like "Have you eaten?" and "I won't take no for an answer; I'll fix you a sandwich."

20. You look in the mirror and see one of your parents peering back at you.

21. Noodles do not form the bulk of your shopping list.

22. You're secretly pleased not to be expected to stay up after midnight on New Year's Eve.

23. You like the idea of curling up with a good book on a Saturday night.

24. You really look forward to your monthly poker games with "the boys," where you eat sensible snacks and play for small amounts of cash.

25. The latest fashions look suspiciously similar to the moth-eaten childhood clothes you keep in a box in the attic.

26. You appreciate the health and social benefits of joining a badminton league.

27. Seventeen-year-olds and twenty-seven-year-olds all look pretty much the same to you: young.

28. You realize that Grandma was right: Knitting *is* fun.

29. Most of your jokes are about how very ancient you are.

30. You secretly hope to be strip-searched at the airport.

> And in the end, it's not the years in your life that count. It's the life in your years.
>
> —*Abraham Lincoln*

Enjoy These Other Reader's Digest Best Sellers

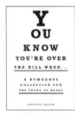